"The loss of a loved one to suicide is, among all other losses, uniquely blistering: it can be fraught with feelings of guilt, rejection, shame, isolation. Living in the wake of her mother's suicide, Rhonda Mawhood Lee shares hard-won wisdom in this pastorally sensitive and theologically informed book. She unflinchingly stares down the horror of suicide by affirming that the mercy of God extends to those who die at their own hand. In a time when even preteen suicides are on the rise, this book is a must read for clergy who will, no doubt at some point, face a suicide in their own flock."

—**Kathryn Greene-McCreight,** author of *Darkness Is My Only Companion: A Christian Response to Mental Illness*

"Vivid, this book is. Searing. Learned. Compassionate. Wise. And perhaps oddly, given the gravity of the topic, reading *Suicide and the Communion of Saints* is—I won't say 'pleasurable,' but deeply satisfying, in that rare way that only reading something true, important, and translucent to the light of Jesus can be."

—**Lauren F. Winner,** Duke Divinity School

"Offering a more healing Christian approach to suicide, Rhonda Mawhood Lee's book is both compassionate and honest in equal measure. For anybody pondering the theological implications of suicide, I wholeheartedly recommend this book. It is a balm for the soul."

—**Elizabeth Antus,** Georgetown University

"Suicide is a mixture of what we can never fully know about ourselves and one another, and what we wish

trust about forever and God. Rhonda Mawhood Lee embraces the former and articulates the latter in a care-full, compassionate, and compelling way. This study plumbs the depths of what suicide means but rises with the glory of who God still is."

—**Samuel Wells,** St. Martin-in-the-Fields

"Like many people, my family and faith community have been affected by suicide. This book is an invaluable resource for those who have questions about the theological implications of suicide, including the role of sin and grace. I strongly recommend this book to anyone—including clergy and lay leaders—as essential reading as we continue to seek a faith-based response to the growing epidemic of suicide both within the US and around the world."

—**Kate H. Rademacher,** author of
Reclaiming Rest: The Promise of Sabbath, Solitude, and Stillness in a Restless World

Suicide and the Communion of Saints

RHONDA MAWHOOD LEE

WILLIAM B. EERDMANS PUBLISHING COMPANY
GRAND RAPIDS, MICHIGAN

Wm. B. Eerdmans Publishing Co.
2006 44th Street SE, Grand Rapids, MI 49508
www.eerdmans.com

© 2025 Rhonda Mawhood Lee
All rights reserved
Published 2025

Book design by Lydia Hall

Printed in the United States of America

31 30 29 28 27 26 25   1 2 3 4 5 6 7

ISBN 978-0-8028-8471-8

Library of Congress Cataloging-in-Publication Data

A catalog record for this book is available from the Library of Congress.

Contents

Forewarning vii

Introduction:
 Called Home, or Duped by the Devil 1

PART ONE: SUICIDE, SIN, AND GRACE

1. How We Talk about Suicide 13
2. Suicide and the Bible 19
3. Augustine and Thomas 32
4. Unforeseen Consequences 41
5. Sinful Settings 49

PART TWO: THE COMMUNION OF SAINTS

6. The Suicidal Christian 61
7. Suicide and the Communion of Saints 71
8. Remembering God's People Who Die by Suicide 86

Contents

Questions to Consider   99
Acknowledgments   103
Notes   105
Bibliography   119
Further Resources   127

Forewarning

If you have picked up this book, you have some connection to both suicide and Christianity. In one sense, everyone is affected by suicide. A country can't lose over forty-eight thousand people a year to suicide, as the United States currently does, without significant ripple effects and collateral damage.[1] Suicide's toll spans the globe: the World Health Organization estimates about 700,000 people kill themselves annually.[2] For some of us, the crisis is especially personal: those who have attempted suicide, or whose family member or friend has attempted or completed suicide. Christians affected by suicide may find that our faith helps us make sense of self-inflicted death, and gives us hope. Or our faith may leave us in despair, causing us to shrink from asking questions whose possible answers we fear. Questions like, "Is my loved one in hell?" or "How could someone who taught me to love Jesus do this?" or "How dare you tell me suicide is a sin?" We may feel defensive on behalf of the deceased when fellow Christians assume a lack of faith or courage was the root cause of their death. We may be left unsatisfied by assumptions that suicide is simply the foreseeable result of a struggle with depression, or of some painful event like the loss of a job.

Forewarning

Because suicide is so emotionally and ethically challenging, I have two introductory notes to offer about this book.

First, a warning. If you are recently bereaved through suicide, today is probably not the day to read this book. In this stage of your journey, contemplating questions of sin and grace, and reading accounts of suicidal despair, is not likely to be helpful. Instead, this is a time to care for yourself and let others care for you; to sit with your feelings and eventually explore them, accompanied by people who love you, perhaps a survivors' support group, and caregiving professionals. This advice comes from my own experience of the healing process. For me, the first year or so after my mother's suicide was a time to sit with friends who simply listened without prying or judging. It was a time to see a therapist weekly, to receive therapeutic massage as often as possible, and to keep up my practice of martial arts. And it was a time to enjoy saganaki, a huge salad, and white wine at my local Greek restaurant where the waiter pretended not to notice that I cried my way through that same meal, once a week, for months. (It may have helped that I tipped him 100 percent, every time.) I have been living with suicide since my mother's first attempt when I was twelve years old, and I expect to be sifting through the implications of my family's generations of self-inflicted death for the rest of my life. Not every resource has been helpful in every moment of my many phases of healing. When the time is right for you, this book will still be available. And if you are what is called a secondary survivor of suicide—say, a friend or pastor to a person bereaved by suicide—please remember this warning and use discretion in suggesting resources to the direct survivor.

Second, a note about scope. This book focuses on the kind of death that is often termed a "despair suicide": a deliberately self-inflicted death in response to psychic pain the person finds

Forewarning

unbearable, sometimes combined with intolerable life circumstances. My discussion does not include other "deaths of despair" (as they are often called), such as car crashes or drug overdoses that cannot clearly be ruled a suicide, or deaths attributed to conditions like substance use disorders. Nor do I address the separate but related ethical issue of physician-assisted death, also known as medical aid in dying or euthanasia. Usually, people who seek physician-assisted suicide have a terminal diagnosis (although the fact that this is not always the case is one reason why this manner of death is controversial). Another key difference between the impact of physician-assisted death and that of despair suicide is that people who seek medical aid in dying often take time to discuss their decision with their family and friends, who may opt to be present at their death. Accordingly, survivors are left with fewer unresolved questions. They may find it easier to understand how, faced with a choice between letting a terminal illness run its course and avoiding the suffering it will bring, their loved one opted for an earlier exit. Deaths of despair and physician-assisted death are important concerns for Christians to ponder, but my focus is narrower.

Who, then, should read this book?

This book is for you if you have lost someone to suicide, you have done some grief work, and you are pondering questions like whether that person is in hell or how a loving God could allow them to perish that way. It will also be helpful if you and your family members have theological disagreements about your loved one's ultimate fate, or if you're wondering about the roots of various Christian views about suicide.

This book is for you, too, if you want to support a friend who is grieving a suicide; if you want to accompany them through their questions, prayers, and healing.

Forewarning

This book may be helpful if you are a Christian who has been suicidal and you are grappling with the church's complicated legacy around self-inflicted death.

Present and future clergy, chaplains, and other church professionals should read this book as preparation for working with people—of all faiths and none—who are bereaved through suicide and with people who are contemplating killing themselves or have attempted it. It will be helpful background for preaching about suicide and the complicated grief that is part of its legacy. You might keep a couple of extra copies ready to offer survivors who approach you with questions several months or years after a friend or family member's death.

Finally, this book is for you if you are a Christian concerned about the growth in suicide rates, who wants to offer thoughtful companionship to the people most directly affected by these deaths, and who wants to respond to suicide in ways informed by Christian tradition.

If you're not ready to read this book, I hope you'll come back to it at a more appropriate time.

If you are ready, thank you for joining me on this journey.

May God bless and guide us all.

Introduction

Called Home, or Duped by the Devil

I met a fellow minister at a work event of the kind that's called a party but that I hardly ever enjoy. There's just too much small talk. So my interest was grabbed when my interlocutor remarked that she had read an essay of mine about my mother's suicide, and that her mother had also killed herself. This was definitely not small talk. I felt the immediate kinship that comes with meeting another member of that sadly not-at-all-exclusive group, survivors of parental suicide. Both of us having lived with a parent who struggled for decades with depression, my acquaintance and I had many experiences in common. But her perspective on her mother's death startled me. She knew her mother had been gripped in her final moments by the deep isolation that people who kill themselves feel. In that profound loneliness, my colleague said, she believed her mother could hear only one voice: God "calling her home." In her view, her mother's suicide was a response to that loving call. And for her, this perspective was deeply comforting.

Contrast her explanation with one offered by Martin Luther.

At dinner with a group of friends, asked whether suicide was a mortal sin, he answered, "It is very certain that, as to all persons who have hanged themselves, or killed themselves in any other

Introduction

way, 'tis the devil who has put the cord round their necks, or the knife to their throats."[1]

Suicide as a response to God's loving call home; suicide as an act of demonic possession. These two interpretations could hardly be more different, and yet they both seek to resolve the same theological problem. How do Christians reckon with the act of deliberate self-destruction? How do we acknowledge that suicide violates God's commandment to value life while we also honor the deep pain that leads people to this end? And how do we grapple with suicide as people who affirm that the end of our earthly life is not the end of our being?

I have struggled with this question as a priest, pastor, and daughter. My mother lived with untreated depression her entire adult life. She attempted suicide more than once when I was a child, and ended her own life when she was fifty-two and I was twenty-eight. In my own middle age, as I explored my family history, I discovered my mother's life had followed a family pattern of depression, suicidal ideation, and self-inflicted death that enmeshed my maternal grandmother, my grandmother's own mother, and several other members of their family. I learned that my biological father, whom I had never met, also died by suicide.[2] I know about complicated grief. I've asked and reasked the questions with unknowable answers. And I'm not alone.

We survivors of suicide typically have complicated emotions about our friend or family member's death. We are shocked, even sickened, by the violence self-destruction embodies, even when the person chooses a bloodless method. We feel compassion for the dead, and we wish our love and care had been enough to save them. We berate ourselves for not having been able to say the right word, offer the right comfort, that could have prevented this tragedy. We wish their earthly story could have ended differently, and we wonder about their eternal fate. We're angry they stopped taking their medication, or wouldn't see a therapist, or rejected the comfort we tried to offer. We resent them for leaving us to carry the load of caring for children or aging parents. We hope they're at peace, and we fear they may not be. Some of us, sometimes, hope they now feel something of the torment they put us through. We bristle at attacks on their memory, or we resent the sympathy for them that seems to leave no room for our anger. We feel relieved that we will no longer have to deal with their illness, their drama, their pushing us away or clutching us too close. We grasp for some logical explanation that will lay our concerns to rest, but all too often there just isn't one. And we wonder where God is in this whole mess.

In the immediate aftermath of a suicide, our questions tend to be concrete: What did he do? Why did she do it? What do I do now? In those early days, police officers, family members, neighbors, clergy, undertakers, lawyers, and insurance agents can help. Of course, their ignorance can also harm or hinder, even when they mean well.

The more challenging questions come later. Where is he now? Can I pray for her? Did God give up on them? Do I have to forgive him—or, on the flip side, do I have to condemn her? How do I help my friend who was bereaved in this way? Can any good come out of this tragedy? If these are the kinds of questions you're asking, I wrote this book to help.

Christians need guidance in thinking about suicide because our emotions about it are so intense and conflicting, and because the church has a problematic history in reckoning with suicide.

It's less common than it used to be to assume that a person who dies by suicide necessarily goes to hell. Today we understand that people who kill themselves usually are in anguish, seeking to end a

Introduction

pain they believe can't be extinguished any other way. What Martin Luther called a demon who placed a cord around someone's neck, you and I might understand as depression or bipolar disorder. A divine Parent who would condemn someone in that situation to eternal punishment is not the God I have met in Jesus Christ.

And yet, suicide remains more complicated, both emotionally and theologically, than we sometimes feel comfortable saying out loud. I often hear suicide described as simply the final stage of a fatal disease. I find that statement both unsatisfying and untrue. Depression is the mental illness most closely associated with suicide, but depression is not typically fatal. Most people with depression never kill themselves (or anyone else). Many other factors can play a role, too, such as stressful life events (like divorce or job loss), substance use disorder, traumatic brain injury, and access to lethal means.[3] Do people who do take their own lives bear any responsibility for that act? What about the people around them, or people with political, cultural, religious, or economic influence over their life? If a trans teenager kills themself to escape the bullying they're experiencing from many quarters, including the church, can their death be attributed to mental illness? Is it a sin? If so, whose sin is it?

If we seek to avoid simplistic accounts, and if Jesus's life, death, and resurrection are the source of any hope we may have, how, then, are Christians to think, pray, and act regarding suicide?

By taking care. If you've read this far, it's likely that something I've written has already made you angry or otherwise touched a nerve—maybe even a nerve you thought had gone numb. That's because suicide is complicated and our feelings about it, even more so. In the face of this complexity, you and I may be tempted to turn to overly simple explanations that spare us from having to examine the pain that is both suicide's motivation and its legacy.

Called Home, or Duped by the Devil

That's an understandable impulse. A friend who is both a faithful Christian and a careful thinker recently asked me, "So, is suicide a sin or not?" That question has governed Christian discussions of suicide for millennia, and it needs reframing. My theological argument about suicide has three parts. First, suicide is a clear and painful sign that we live in a world marked by sin and death. Second, to say that suicide is a marker of sin—that it reveals the distance between the life God wants for us and the shape actual human lives take—is not to pass judgment on any person who dies by suicide. Third, the resurrection of Jesus Christ promises that the power of God is greater than the power of death, and offers hope that we will live again in a state of perfect union with God and each other. The promise of the resurrection affects our earthly life, too, assuring us that freer lives and more loving relationships than we can currently imagine are attainable in this realm.

Christian faith, and the life to which that faith commits us, rests on the resurrection of Jesus. Only a couple of decades after the first Easter, the apostle Paul reminded the church in Corinth that it was the foundation of their lives: "if Christ has not been raised, then our proclamation has been in vain and your faith has been in vain."[4] In Jesus's resurrection, we see our promised future: "in fact Christ has been raised from the dead, the first fruits of those who have died. For since death came through a human being, the resurrection of the dead has also come through a human being; for as all die in Adam, so all will be made alive in Christ."[5]

As we encounter God in Jesus Christ, we know God to be the One who gives life and overcomes death. In Jesus Christ, we see that death has never been God's will for us. Death is a sign and a consequence of living in a fallen world. This world is breathtakingly beautiful—I'm reminded of that as I write these words ac-

Introduction

companied by a choir of birds greeting the spring sunrise—and it is also deeply marked by death.

Suicide is one of the most obvious signs of death's continued power. There are others: murder; capital punishment; the water crisis in Flint, Michigan, and ongoing lack of clean drinking water on Native American reservations; the slowly yet undeniably increasing stiffness of all my joints as I travel through my fifties; my tendency to keep reopening arguments with my spouse after multiple opportunities to reach an agreement, forgive each other, and move on. Christians stake our lives on the promise of the resurrection, and also, we constantly deny resurrection's power and give in to the lure of death. Suicide is one of the most obvious ways in which human beings do that, often because this fallen world has laid unbearable burdens on them. Whereas God the Creator brings life into being for love's sake, suicide is de-creation, the destruction of life that God has engendered.

Too much Christian theological discourse around suicide has revolved around sin in a different way, focusing on whether or not to attach blame to the person who dies. Until recently, the dominant strain of Christian thought has been that suicide is a mortal sin, by which the person condemns themself to hell. In part 1, we will examine some of those arguments, and also see that they were never as fully accepted as Christians have typically imagined.

When speaking theologically of suicide, to focus on blame is to miss the point. It is unmistakably true that suicide harms survivors. Suicide attempts harm the people who care about the person who tried to die. Suicide tears holes in the web of caring relationships we weave with God's help. When the person who has been suicidal is stable enough emotionally that they are able to hear how their attempts have harmed others, it's appropriate to speak that truth. The fact that suicide is often related to mental illness or past trauma does not change the harm done by suicide, although it does make motivations more complex and demonstrate the futility of assigning blame.

To say that suicide reveals sin—embodies it, even—is not the same as presuming to know the ultimate fate of the person who dies in this way. Christians can still trust that the suicidal person is in God's care, and we can still hope they will live again, as all Christians hope to. Paul's words about living in a state of sin apply to all of us: "I do not understand my own actions. For I do not do what I want, but I do the very thing I hate."[6] For the suicidal person, the chilling reality is that the power of sin manifests itself in them as the drive to end their own existence. As comedian John Mulaney has put it, "When I'm alone, I realize I'm with the person who tried to kill me."[7]

Rather than focusing on whether suicide is an individual sin or not, for which the person who dies should be held accountable or not, I invite you to think of suicide as one deeply painful manifestation of the reality that we live in a fallen world marked by sin and death. Christians are called to resist suicide as we are called to resist other manifestations of sin, and I believe the power of the resurrected Jesus Christ is with us as we do so. I also believe that as sinners who depend wholly on God's grace for our salvation—that is, for our present and future healing and liberation—none of us is in a position to condemn a fellow child of God who dies by suicide.

Death is never God's will for us. Christians affirm that human beings are created to share in God's life; that God shared our life in the person of Jesus Christ; and that our own earthly life is shaped by the hope of full communion with God and each other one day. For a Christian to deliberately end their own life negates

Introduction

those affirmations; and for a person of any faith or no faith to do so is a deep loss for the human community. And yet, I trust that God deeply loves those who die by suicide, just as I hope God also continues to love me when my actions betray my claim to be a disciple of Jesus.

I wrote this book to accompany fellow Christians who are ready to think and pray about suicide differently, and who want to find and offer hope to people affected by suicide. Because our lives are inextricably interwoven through Jesus Christ, Christians need always to think about suicide within the context of our relationships with God and each other. On a fundamental level, we are all in this together, whether or not suicide touches us directly.

James Baldwin understood this. He fled the United States for Paris in 1948 because, as he remarked decades later, as a Black American man, "My luck was running out. I was going to jail, I was going to kill somebody or be killed."[8] The "somebody" he would have killed might have been himself. Baldwin attempted suicide more than once, and one of the motivators for his exile was the death of his dear friend Eugene Worth in 1946. Worth was the model for Rufus, a main character in Baldwin's 1962 novel *Another Country* who, like Baldwin's friend, leaps off the George Washington Bridge.

At different times in his life, Rufus has been homeless, forced by economic circumstance into sex work, variously appreciated and objectified by white men and women alike. Broken by love, racked by guilt, abandoned by his friends, Rufus takes the only step he imagines is still open to him.

The pastor who preaches Rufus's funeral sermon refuses to judge him. "He had his trouble and he's gone," Reverend Foster

Called Home, or Duped by the Devil

says of the man he had watched grow from boyhood. Reverend Foster acknowledges his own pain, and that of his congregation: "I know how terrible I feel—ain't nothing I can say going to take away that ache, not right away." And then he urges compassion and solidarity for their fellow child of God: "You know, a lot of people say that a man who takes his own life oughtn't to be buried in holy ground. I don't know nothing about that.... And don't none of us know what goes on in the heart of someone . . . and so can't none of us say why he did what he did.... We got to pray that the Lord will receive him like we pray that the Lord's going to receive us. That's all. That's *all*."[9]

The rest of this book is divided into two parts.

In part 1, we will gain some insights into how Christians have understood self-inflicted death from the early centuries of the church through the present. We will consider the unintended consequences of certain Christian teachings around suicide, and the role context has played in leading people to kill themselves. We will see that Christians have long argued about suicide, its causes, and how to respond to it.

In part 2, we will explore the concept of the communion of saints and how it could be employed to reimagine our relationships with people who have died by suicide, and with those of us who are in danger of dying that way. We will consider what it might mean to stay in relationship with both the living and the dead, Christians and non-Christians, as a witness to our hope and faith in God's creative and redemptive love.

My discussion of suicide is not comprehensive. The ideas and stories I present here are meant to be evocative and thought provoking, a spur to prayers and actions that feel faithful to you. Hav-

Introduction

ing written this book specifically for Christians, I hope it will not only spark conversations within the church but will also allow us to engage with people of other faiths and no faith in mutually respectful conversations and in cooperative action where possible. Not all Christians believe, think, or practice just alike. My perspective is shaped by myriad realities, including the fact that I am a North American citizen of European descent; a middle-class person raised by people who, like their ancestors, grew up in poverty; and a priest in the Episcopal Church. I hope, however, that the core beliefs presented here will resonate with believers from across Christ's diverse church, and I hope this book will serve as a springboard to further discussions of belief and practice within your own particular tradition.

To help you engage with and respond to the material presented here, I have written questions for each chapter for you to ponder. These are printed at the end of the book. You can contemplate them on your own or with a friend or study group; you can let them be if they don't seem helpful or if you're not ready for them. However you interact with this book, I trust the Holy Spirit will guide you, and I pray you will find something you need.

PART ONE

Suicide, Sin, and Grace

CHAPTER ONE

How We Talk about Suicide

When my maternal grandmother spoke of suicide, she called it "self-murder." As in, "How did he die?" "He murdered himself." Born in 1918 and raised in the Church of Scotland, she had been inculcated with a detailed list of sinful behaviors to avoid and given no way to think of suicide other than as a wicked and willful act of self-destruction.

Even before my mother died, I never liked hearing my grandmother talk about self-murder. I found the term judgmental and lacking in compassion. But as a young adult, I came to realize there may have been a benefit to her harsh belief. It may have helped keep her alive. From time to time, my grandmother would tell me of her desire to throw herself into the North Sea, along whose shores she walked daily, or to wash down a bottle of acetaminophen with the brandy she kept in a kitchen cabinet for my grandfather's angina attacks. As I paid attention to what she did and didn't say, I gleaned that two fears pulled her up short. She didn't want to bring shame upon her family, and she was convinced that to leap into the sea, or into the bottle, would be to launch herself into hell. The eternal torments she believed awaited her would be immeasurably more painful than the suffering she longed to leave behind.

Part One. Suicide, Sin, and Grace

This is the paradox I sit with: what I considered a cruel and theologically dubious belief may have saved my grandmother's life. I'll never know for sure; people who experience suicidal ideation don't necessarily move on to attempting suicide. But the strong moral opprobrium around suicide that was part of her upbringing definitely governed her thinking on the topic, and may well have kept her from moving on to attempting it.

My grandmother died of cancer at eighty-five, but her long life was a mixed blessing. She outlived her daughter, my mother, by almost a decade. The same harsh belief that had more than once convinced my grandmother to spare her own life made it excruciating, in her final years, to contemplate her child's fate. My grandmother's pain over her daughter's death was hard to witness. I never found a way to bridge the chasm of belief between us: between my conviction that my mother was no longer suffering and her terror that her daughter was being eternally punished. And, traumatized by events in her own childhood as well as the loss of her daughter, curved inward on her own pain, my grandmother was never able to express compassion for my loss, nor to seek fellowship in shared suffering.

I came to a deeper understanding of my grandmother's pain after she herself died. Finally doing the genealogical research she had always forbidden, I learned that her daughter's death was not the only one my grandmother had grieved. I came to understand why she would never talk about her family, and how many secrets she had worked hard to keep hidden. Her own mother had died in 1924, hours after having been committed to a mental hospital, leaving five children between the ages of eight years and six months. My grandmother, at six, was the second oldest. Very likely a suicide, my great-grandmother's death was not labeled as such. That doesn't mean much, as compassionate doctors have

How We Talk about Suicide

often refrained from ruling deaths suicides if at all possible, to spare the deceased and their family shame. But her withdrawal into whatever disease caused her to be deemed "insane," her institutionalization, and her immediate death taught her children that emotional troubles were not only dangerous but also too shameful to talk about. Even their mother's name was no longer safe to utter. My grandmother said it to me only once, in response to my direct question, and my own mother warned me never to ask about that lost great-grandmother.

The effects of my great-grandmother's death have reverberated through our family for generations. Their widowed father unable to care for them, my grandmother and her four siblings were removed to foster care hundreds of miles north of their birthplace, Glasgow. Poor, repeatedly traumatized, with no opportunity to tell and retell their stories and thus make some sense of what had happened to them, at least one and likely two of the siblings died by suicide. Of their children's—my mother's—generation, at least two killed themselves while at least one more attempted. Even after the family moved out of desperate poverty and its stresses, the stigma attached to mental illness and suicide led our family to deny both our trauma and our genetic inheritance. And that denial was rooted in unhelpful theology.

I don't think my grandmother or her teachers in the faith were wrong to recoil from suicide. God's sovereignty over life and death is something for Christians to take seriously; arguments over war, the death penalty, and abortion reckon with this fundamental principle. And yet, terms like "self-murder" pass judgment in a way that I and many other Christians find inappropriate and distasteful. This turn of phrase takes into account neither the illness nor the circumstances that may drive a person to suicide, nor God's deep compassion for our human frailty. In

Part One. Suicide, Sin, and Grace

thinking theologically about suicide, reflecting on the words we use is a helpful place to start.

When I speak of my mother's death, I never say she "committed" suicide. I say she died by suicide, or she killed herself. That's because the word "commit" implies that the act is a sin, a crime, or both. I don't want to put that kind of judgment on my mother, or anyone, through the simple act of sharing the manner of her death.

The English term "commit suicide" makes it particularly clear that the word "suicide" has been inseparable from Christian thought. Theologians invented it specifically for the purpose of condemning the act.[1] Although the act of suicide has been documented for thousands of years, the word "suicide" itself, as used in European languages like English, French, and Spanish, has only existed for a few centuries. (It seems that words from cultures that have never been majority-Christian are typically more neutral, such as the Japanese *jisatsu*, which simply means "self-killing," without the connotation of a moral or legal offense.) Other than one known use by the French theologian Gauthier de Saint-Victor in the twelfth century, who seemed to believe he was coining a new term, the neo-Latin term *suicidium* seems to have originated in the seventeenth century. It only became common in the eighteenth.[2]

Earlier generations of Christians don't seem to have felt the need for such a specific word. Writing in the early fifth century, Augustine of Hippo simply referred to people who "killed themselves." When he wanted to make the act's moral gravity clear, he stated bluntly that "anyone who kills himself is a murderer."[3] The

How We Talk about Suicide

Latin word translated as "murderer" was *homicida*—"homicide." In Augustine's time, as in our own, that term did not always imply the culpability associated with willful murder, but the context makes his disapproval clear.

It was early modern European theologians who invented the word "suicide." They were undeterred by the fact that their neologism was "simply horrendously bad Latin," as historian Anton van Hooff says; *suicidium* could as easily be read as "sow [female pig]-killer" as "self-killer."[4] English speakers had already been using the term "self-murder" since the sixteenth century, according to the *Oxford English Dictionary*, as well as the Latin *felo de se* (literally, guilty concerning oneself). Theologians who wrote in Latin seem, however, to have wanted a Latin word that would specifically denote the act of killing oneself, while also conveying moral opprobrium.

Today, the word "suicide" can be used in ways that condemn or stay relatively neutral as long as it's not twinned with the verb "commit." That's why I say my mother died by suicide; it's as neutral a phrase as I can use to describe a deeply complicated death. Other options are to say someone "took their own life" or "killed themself." We might also say someone "completed suicide" to make a distinction between attempting suicide, but it's jarring—and to me, distasteful—to read of a "successful suicide" or "unsuccessful attempt."[5] I'm not alone in this. In its guidelines for responsible reporting on suicide, the American Foundation for Suicide Prevention addresses the importance of language, stating, "Do not refer to a suicide attempt as 'successful,' 'unsuccessful' or as a 'failed attempt,' and do not use the word 'committed.' Instead, use 'attempted suicide,' 'made an attempt,' 'died by suicide' or 'took his/her life.'"[6]

Part One. Suicide, Sin, and Grace

As you read on in this book, you will encounter a variety of words that make a number of judgments about suicide. I invite you to notice the thoughts and feelings that come up for you as you read them, and then to take those thoughts and feelings, as well as the ideas presented here, into your own discernment about how to think and speak about suicide.

CHAPTER TWO

Suicide and the Bible

Scripture is one of the primary resources to which Christians turn for guidance. As is the case with many twenty-first-century concerns, however, the Bible says little directly about suicide. We can't, then, turn to it for easy answers, but we can use it as an instructive, authoritative resource that will help us, in community with other Christians, to be more faithful in our words and deeds.

Undergirding the traditional Christian lamentation of suicide is the fact that the Bible holds human life in high esteem. The ninth chapter of Genesis warns, "Whoever sheds the blood of a human, by a human shall that person's blood be shed; for in his own image God made humankind."[1] This provision can't apply literally to suicide, because in a suicide the person shedding blood and the victim are the same. But it does speak to the value of human life: that God's people are not to destroy what is made in the image of God. (That's one of the reasons this passage can't be taken simplistically as an argument for capital punishment: convicted murderers, like their victims, are made in God's image.) The sixth commandment, "You shall not murder,"[2] forbids intentional and illicit taking of life, although Christian Bibles often follow the King James translation

Part One. Suicide, Sin, and Grace

in broadening the commandment beyond its original Hebrew meaning to "You shall not kill." As we shall see, the question of whether or not suicide can be construed as "intentional" has long preoccupied Christians.

The fact that the Bible says little overtly about suicide doesn't mean the topic is altogether absent from Scripture. The Old Testament contains a handful of accounts of suicide or deaths that could be construed as suicide. Although suicide itself is condemned in none of the stories, the pain and ignominy of these deaths are striking. The short-lived king Abimelech is targeted for assassination by "a certain woman," who throws a millstone and crushes his skull. The king commands his armor-bearer, "Draw your sword and kill me, so people will not say about me, 'A woman killed him.'"[3] Another king of Israel, Zimri, when he saw that his seven-day reign was about to be ended by force, locked himself into the royal palace, "burned down the king's house over himself with fire, and died—because of the sins that he committed, doing evil in the sight of the Lord."[4] In both these cases, the biblical narrator suggests not that Abimelech's and Zimri's deaths were themselves sins, but rather that their painful ends were a divine punishment.

Another suicide, that of Ahithophel, is narrated in an entirely matter-of-fact way. Ahithophel, an adviser to King David, took the side of David's son Absalom in his revolt against the king. When Absalom rejects Ahithophel's advice, setting himself up for defeat, the Second Book of Samuel says, Ahithophel "saddled his donkey and went off home to his own city. He set his house in order, and hanged himself; he died and was buried in the tomb of his father."[5] Biblical scholar Robert Alter points out that Ahithophel kills himself not only because "he has lost face," but also because he is sure to be executed for treason when King David returns to his throne. "Thus," Alter notes, "in tying the noose around his own neck, [Ahithophel] anticipates the executioner's sword."[6] As in the stories of Abimelech and Zimri, Ahithophel's suicide is, itself, a judgment on him, not an act for which he is to be judged.

A more ambiguous case is the death of Samson. Once a hero in Israel's conflict with the Philistines, he loses his legendary strength when his lover Delilah—a Philistine spy—shaves his head. Shorn, weakened, blinded by his enemies, mocked, and forced to play music at a celebratory sacrifice to the Philistines' god, Samson asks for God's strength to flow through him once more. "Lord God, remember me and strengthen me only this once . . . so that with this one act of revenge I may pay back the Philistines for my two eyes." Samson plainly understands that his own death will be the price of vengeance, as he states, "Let me die with the Philistines."[7] For whatever reason, God grants Samson the strength he seeks and Samson pushes apart the temple's central pillars, bringing down the structure on his own head and the heads of thousands of his enemies.[8]

The narrator makes it clear that Samson's motivation is revenge. He is not actively seeking his own death; nor does he focus on the fact that his act of mass killing will help his nation in their struggle against the Philistines. His death, then, could be counted as a personal vendetta to which both suicide and military considerations are incidental. Despite this, the Christian tradition remembers Samson as a hero. The Letter to the Hebrews names him among the faithful of old: "And what more should I say? For time would fail me to tell of Gideon, Barak, Samson, Jephthah, of David and Samuel and the prophets—who through faith conquered kingdoms, administered justice, obtained promises, shut the mouths of lions, quenched raging fire, escaped the edge of the sword, won strength out of weakness, be-

Part One. Suicide, Sin, and Grace

came mighty in war, put foreign armies to flight."[9] Along with soldiers fighting a just war and executioners carrying out a sentence imposed by due authority, Samson is specifically mentioned by Augustine as an exception to God's law against homicide. "When Samson destroyed himself, with his enemies, by the demolition of the building," Augustine wrote in *City of God*, "this can only be excused on the ground that the Spirit, which performed miracles through him, secretly ordered him to do so."[10] Augustine's view of Samson was likely colored by Roman Christians' fear of conquest by pagan invaders, and by his generation's interest in defining the line between suicide and martyrdom; we will consider those concerns in the next chapter.

Although the Bible doesn't present suicide in a positive light, some of its writers clearly understood the urge to self-annihilation. Perhaps the clearest example is what literary scholar and biblical translator Robert Alter calls the "harrowing death-wish poem" found in the book of Job.[11] His children dead, his wealth burned up, his skin afire, Job curses his life thoroughly and repeatedly. He cries,

> "Let the day perish in which I was born,
>   and the night that said,
>   'A man-child is conceived.'"

"Why," Job wonders, "did I not die at birth, come forth from the womb and expire?" And why does death refuse to come for him now, Job demands to know, in words that resonate with suicidal souls:

Suicide and the Bible

> "Why is light given to one in misery,
> and life to the bitter in soul,
> who long for death, but it does not come,
> and dig for it more than for hidden treasures;
> who rejoice exceedingly,
> and are glad when they find the grave?"

Job longs for death because he has found that in life,

> "Truly the thing that I fear comes upon me,
> and what I dread befalls me."[12]

In the grave, this grievously afflicted man believes, his suffering would be blotted out. Job does not attempt to end his life, but the fact that his overwhelming desire to die is included in the canon of Scripture might comfort some who share his wish. Deeply—even emblematically—faithful souls have experienced their distress.

Recently, I heard a passage from Paul's letter to the Philippians read in church, and his words hit me differently than ever before. "For to me living is Christ and dying is gain," the apostle wrote from prison. "If I am to live in the flesh, that means fruitful labor for me; and I do not know which I prefer. I am hard pressed between the two: my desire is to depart and be with Christ, for that is far better; but to remain in the flesh is more necessary for you."[13] I wondered for the first time whether Paul had ever considered suicide. Investigating my question, I learned that a minority of biblical scholars have argued that Paul was tempted

Part One. Suicide, Sin, and Grace

to suicide, and that while he decided against it in the moment, he retained it as an option should his circumstances warrant.[14]

More convincingly, however, and emphasizing the benefit Paul sees in suffering for and with Christ, N. Clayton Croy has argued that in this letter, Paul used "a rhetorical trope known as ... 'feigned perplexity,'" posing a question "as a way of strengthening or dramatizing an argument."[15] By allowing for the possibility that he might accept death—not necessarily by suicide but possibly by not mounting a defense at his trial—Paul is framing the choices before him to show that he is taking the better path by preserving his life and remaining with his siblings in Christ.

We have no way of knowing whether Paul ever contemplated suicide in the midst of his hardships. As Croy points out, we don't know whether he would have condoned suicide under any circumstances. It's unclear whether Christians had yet specifically taken up the question of whether suicide might ever be justified.[16] What we do see in Paul's letter to the Philippians is a commitment to abide with his friends for the sake of Jesus Christ.

In the Christian tradition, suicide is inextricably linked to Judas. Among many others, Augustine cited him as the definitive example of self-inflicted death. "We rightly abominate the act of Judas," Augustine wrote; "when Judas killed himself, he killed a criminal, and yet he ended his life guilty not only of Christ's death, but also of his own; one crime led to another."[17] In her *Dialogues* between God and the human soul a millennium later, theologian and mystic Catherine of Siena quotes God as denouncing the logic of people who kill themselves "in judging her [i.e., the soul's] misery greater than My [i.e., God's] mercy." For this reason, according to Catherine's vision of God, "the de-

Suicide and the Bible

spair of Judas displeased Me more, and was more grave to My Son than was his betrayal of Him."[18] According to Augustine and Catherine, Judas did not expiate his guilt by killing himself in remorse over betraying Jesus. Rather, he compounded it. For all we know, Judas might agree with their judgment. Certainly, modern people who have left suicide notes have expressed remorse for what they are about to do. My mother wrote, "Please forgive me if I have hurt you this is not a reflection on anyone." She was normally meticulous about punctuation, so the fact that she ran all her words together in her final communication shows her single-minded focus on moving toward what she believed she must do. Given that I had never once before heard her ask for forgiveness, I have to think she was referring specifically to the fact that her manner of death might hurt those of us she left behind. She made no plea for the rightness of what she was about to do.

Christians don't know for sure that Judas killed himself. Our assumption that he did comes from just one poignant passage in Matthew's Gospel: "When Judas, his betrayer, saw that Jesus was condemned, he repented and brought back the thirty pieces of silver to the chief priests and the elders. He said, 'I have sinned by betraying innocent blood.' But they said, 'What is that to us? See to it yourself.' Throwing down the pieces of silver in the temple, he departed; and he went and hanged himself."[19] In artwork from as early as the fifth century, images abound of Judas dangling from a tree, alone or with the devil nearby, sometimes with his blood money scattered beneath his feet.

Often overlooked is the fact that Matthew is the only New Testament writer to say Judas killed himself. The narrator of Acts describes his death as an act of divine judgment, saying Judas "acquired a field with the reward of his wickedness; and falling headlong, he burst open in the middle and all his bowels

Part One. Suicide, Sin, and Grace

gushed out."[20] The two manners of death seem physically incompatible (although some have tried to reconcile them, suggesting that Judas's rope broke and he fell forward onto rocks, thus being gashed open).

Regardless of how Judas died, the evangelists remember him primarily not for his possible suicide but rather for his betrayal of Jesus. In their lists of Jesus's apostles, every gospel writer including Matthew identifies him as "the one who betrayed" the Lord, or in Luke's case, "the one who became a traitor." This suggests that Judas's greatest sin was not his suicide but leading Jesus's executioners to him.

The medieval poet Dante certainly thought so. In his *Inferno*, Dante places Judas, not among the souls who had killed themselves, but in the very deepest circle of hell, the place farthest from God, reserved for those who had betrayed their lords and benefactors. Shoved headfirst into Satan's own mouth, Judas's fate is to be continually and repeatedly crushed between the devil's teeth.[21] Judas is personally punished by the one whom tradition remembers as the first traitor to God. Dante's harsh judgment of Judas may have been colored by his own experience of politics, war, and intrigue in his native city-state of Florence, which he had to flee in fear for his life after his side lost a civil war. In Dante's time, social and political order depended greatly on what medieval historian Alexander Murray calls "man-to-man loyalty."[22] In Dante's context, the gospel writers' characterizations of Judas as a traitor would have resonated particularly strongly.

Christian judgments of Judas have not been rooted purely in his betrayal of Jesus and his self-inflicted death. They have also been inextricable from the church's anti-Judaism. In the late Middle Ages, as European Christians consciously self-differentiated from people of other faiths; as Jews were barred from most professions and from owning land; and as Christian moral theology condemned the practice of lending money at interest, the figure of Judas was the symbolic target par excellence of anti-Judaism. As Alexander Murray notes, not only did artists include Judas's thirty pieces of silver in their depictions of him, they also clothed him in the yellow garments that Christian governments increasingly required of Jews after 1300.[23] In that context, Judas's alleged suicide made him an easy scapegoat to burden with Christian anti-Jewish stereotypes. Persons discussing Judas now must keep in mind the long tradition of anti-Judaism intertwined with Christian portrayals of him, and be careful not to reinforce those prejudices.

Today, theologian and biblical scholar Willie James Jennings reminds the church that none of us is Judas's judge, nor can we be certain of his fate. In his commentary on Acts, in the first chapter, where Peter characterizes Judas as a betrayer whose bad end was foretold, Jennings notes that "the last word on Judas will not come from Peter. It will come from Jesus." That is both good news and a caution. Much like the first disciples, Christians today are still trying to come to grips with the resurrection "and what it means for how we speak of those who have died in shame, died in pain, died in guilt." With all due respect to Peter, Augustine, Aquinas, Catherine of Siena, and all who might seek the last word on Judas's death or anyone else's, Jennings's caution is appropriate. "Last words no longer belong to us," he writes. "They have been seized by a savior. Jesus' power now reaches into the grave, into Judas's grave."[24] I trust this is true for Judas and for all of us, however we may have sinned, however we might die.

Part One. Suicide, Sin, and Grace

Beyond the places where it mentions death by suicide, how can the Bible expand Christians' imaginations as we reckon with suicide?

Catholic theologian Jessica Coblentz has shared ways in which the story of Hagar resonates with her as a person who has suffered from major depression. By extension, it may be helpful for those who have contemplated suicide. Hagar is the young Egyptian woman, enslaved by Abraham and Sarah, who at Sarah's request bears Abraham's first son, Ishmael. The book of Genesis includes two stories of Hagar. In both, the reader encounters her in the wilderness where she and her son face virtually certain death. In the first story, Hagar has run away to escape Sarah's harsh treatment, and in the second, Abraham has cast her out at Sarah's request.[25] Alone, abandoned, with no kin or community to support her (Hagar's very name can mean "the stranger" in Hebrew), Hagar encounters God, who hears her, sees her, and reassures her that she and her son have a meaningful future, with "offspring . . . [who] cannot be counted for multitude."[26]

For Coblentz, "depressive suffering" can be seen as an analogue to Hagar's story. Hagar is cast into the wilderness through no fault of her own, apparently with God's approval (or at least, without God intervening). But in that wilderness, God sees her and calls out to her. Hagar affirms this reality by becoming the first person in the Bible to name God: El-Roi, "God Who Sees." Her son Ishmael's name has already affirmed that "God Hears." Coblentz notes, "Hagar's suffering matters to God. God is present to it. And yet the telling of her story presents no theological justification for this suffering." No deeper meaning is offered. Likewise, when we suffer without any discernible purpose or meaning, our pain matters to "the God who is profoundly concerned with and attentive to the suffering and the distraught."[27]

Coblentz acknowledges that, while God intervenes to help Hagar and Ishmael survive—and Ishmael goes on to father a nation—"God's intervention does not explain why she has suffered or goes on suffering."[28] In that sense, Hagar's story has a tragic dimension, even as it offers "a portrait of a personal and life-giving God who is concerned with those who suffer."[29] I suspect that even this tragic dimension could be helpful to those who have felt themselves cast into metaphorical desert places. Tragedy is part of life, and it can be contained within our ultimate Christian hope of redemption. The fact that biblical stories don't have smooth, happy endings, nor deny the suffering that life brings, is part of what makes them resonate in our own painful or messy situations.

For people in the throes of suicidal ideation or related crises, some images and conceptions of God may be more helpful than others. David Finnegan-Hosey notes that when he was hospitalized for bipolar disorder, the image of God as "a distant king, or even a rarely available doctor, only worked to exacerbate my suffering." More accessible images, of "God as a companion, healer, or caretaker," touched him. He went on, "[They] were able to get in underneath my pain and shore up my fragile sense that I was not alone and that I might even be able to survive at all."[30] Lauren F. Winner has explored a plethora of biblical images of God that might resonate with people in suicidal distress: God who runs after our friendship; God as clothing, which might be comforting like an old cozy sweater, or protective like

Part One. Suicide, Sin, and Grace

armor (or an aptly named "power suit"); God as bread, which the depressed person might not want to eat but whose aroma as it bakes might evoke a pleasurable memory and maybe even something resembling appetite.[31]

None of these images should be imposed on a suffering person, but they could be offered by a caring friend in faith.

The Bible testifies that Jesus, like countless other human beings, wrestled with thoughts of death. A Christian who finds themself in that position might find companionship in Jesus, who prayed at Gethsemane as he felt death drawing nearer. Jesus implored God to "remove this cup from [him]," even as he accepted that his role in accomplishing God's purposes might take him to the cross.[32] And one who feels forsaken by God might find comfort in biblical evidence of Jesus having felt that kind of deep desolation on the cross.

It is true, however, that a suicidal person might be more likely to invoke Jesus's acceptance of death than would a companion seeking to keep them alive. A suicidal person might see death as God's will for them. They might see Jesus's promise to the man who was crucified with him, "Today you will be with me in Paradise," as a hopeful reason to put an end to their earthly sufferings.

In light of this, I think it's important to note that Jesus never sought out death. Rather, he accepted it as a consequence of human sin—sin in which he did not share—and of the divine willingness to bear the cost of human sinfulness.

Jesus wasn't suicidal. But he does know what it's like to live with the possibility of death as a near companion, to feel death lurking, to sense that he will meet it sooner rather than later. And

Suicide and the Bible

he knows the experience of feeling utterly abandoned by God. Jesus, who prayed for the cup of anguish to pass from him, who cried out, "My God, why have you forsaken me?" is a tender ally for those who find themselves fighting the illusion that death is a more faithful friend than is God the Creator of life.

Scripture is one of the most vital resources for developing Christian theology and ethics. However, theologians writing about suicide have mined it more for general principles than for specific stories about self-inflicted death, and their biblical interpretations have been deeply influenced by their contexts and their pastoral sensitivities. Their theological explorations of suicide, in turn, have had a more lasting impact on the church than any biblical narrative.

CHAPTER THREE

Augustine and Thomas

Augustine of Hippo and Thomas Aquinas are the two theologians most closely associated with Christian opprobrium around suicide. Living almost a millennium apart, they developed their ideas about suicide within quite different theological projects, but they shared a pastoral concern: that Christians should not give up on either life or God's grace. Augustine's and Thomas's pastoral sensibilities are frequently forgotten in discussions of their views about suicide, and I think that's unfortunate. Appreciating certain nuances of their arguments can help twenty-first-century people realize that some of our concerns were also theirs.

Augustine is remembered for teaching explicitly that suicide was "forbidden by the law 'You shall not kill.'"[1] As we consider Augustine's views about suicide, it's important to know two things about his context. First, Augustine was participating in one of the most intense Christian theological debates of the fifth century, writing forcefully against the Donatists. That sect's desire for a morally pure church was so fervent that some of its members sought out martyrdom or killed themselves after a life of self-denial, the sooner to escape this sinful world and live with God and the saints. As we saw in the previous chapter, Augustine did acknowledge that Christians could be called to martyrdom.

He saw Samson—venerated in Scripture—as one valid example. For Augustine, however, Samson acted on the specific instruction of the Holy Spirit, while the vast majority of Christians would never be in that position.

Second, Augustine developed his argument about suicide in the midst of the social upheaval that accompanied the decline of the Roman Empire. Specifically, in making his case against suicide, Augustine wrote about women facing the possibility of being raped by Rome's invaders. He showed pastoral concern for survivors of sexual violence, teaching both that their assailants' sin did not reflect badly on them and also that their lives remained valuable after they had been violated.

In his argument about suicide, Augustine broke with several of his contemporaries, including Ambrose of Milan, the bishop who had catechized and baptized him. Ambrose joined other teachers, like the biblical translator Jerome, in arguing that women who killed themselves when threatened with rape were martyrs worthy of emulation. "Placed," as Ambrose put it, "in the necessity of preserving their purity," these women, he believed, made the most faithful Christian decision.[2]

Augustine took the contrary position in his book *City of God*. He was not the first Christian teacher to condemn the practice of suicide. Lactantius, an apologist and adviser to the emperor Constantine, had taught that suicide was both an unnatural act and also the most severely punished sin, because the person committing it had no earthly opportunity to make amends.[3] But whereas Lactantius was primarily concerned with developing a taxonomy of sins and their appropriate punishments as the church was gaining power, a century later Augustine was developing a pastoral theology for Christians living through a political and social crisis with emotional and theological consequences.

Part One. Suicide, Sin, and Grace

In *City of God*, Augustine opens his argument with a rhetorical question that prioritizes compassion for people threatened with sexual assault: "Even if some of these virgins [i.e., unmarried women threatened with rape] killed themselves to avoid such disgrace, who that has any human feeling would refuse to forgive them?" And yet, while affirming the importance of compassion, Augustine reiterates the church's prohibition of suicide. He reminds his readers that the authority to give and to take life belongs to God.[4] Just as importantly, but not often remembered, Augustine asserts that people who have been sexually violated, or who fear they might be, have no reason to feel ashamed. "They have the glory of chastity within them, the testimony of their conscience"—in other words, they are not responsible for any assault another person might have perpetrated upon them. "They have this [testimony] in the sight of God," and God knows it is true.[5]

As the historian of suicide Alexander Murray notes, Augustine was distinguishing between the values of the relatively new Christian faith and Roman paganism.[6] Rome valorized Lucretia, a noblewoman who, tradition said, killed herself in the sixth century BCE after being raped by the king's son. Her assault and death were remembered as having touched off a rebellion that led to the founding of the Roman republic. Her example of choosing death rather than living with "dishonor" still loomed large in early Christian Rome; it fell to Augustine to remind the faithful that Christians should feel no shame in being the object of another's sin. Being assaulted would naturally cause suffering, but it was no reflection on one's character or the state of one's soul. Rereading Augustine's words now, I have to wonder: How much pain would have been prevented over the centuries if the church had taken to heart Augustine's views on this topic? What if Christians had emphasized the inherent worth of people targeted for assault and tempted to suicide, and God's immeasurable love for them, rather than condemning them for their assailants' sin?

Lucretia was not the only pagan model of virtuous suicide against which Augustine elaborated a distinctive Christian view. The Stoic school of philosophy judged suicide to be noble in a variety of circumstances, including when it was used to avoid being forced by a tyrannical ruler to commit immoral acts. Christians who were influenced by this school of thought argued that it could be not only permissible, but even virtuous, to kill oneself to avoid future sin. Augustine opposed this line of reasoning by following it to an extreme. If avoiding sin were a good reason for Christians to kill themselves, Augustine wrote, the most logical course of action would be to move directly from the baptismal font to suicide. "For that would be the time to forestall all future sins," he jabbed, "the moment at which all past sins have been erased." And if following baptism by suicide did make theological sense, "why should [any baptized person] expose himself again to all the perils of this life, when it is so easily allowed him to avoid them by doing away with himself?"[7] The reason, Augustine affirmed, was that unlike his Donatist opponents, most Christians realized it would be a sin to kill oneself, or to exhort anyone else to end their own life. Instead, Christians are meant to trust in God and our community of faith to help us resist sin, and we are called to confess, receive absolution, and start over when we inevitably fall short. We are indeed created to live with God forever, Augustine affirmed, but we are not meant to seek out that full communion on our own timetable.

Today, the words well-meaning pastors offer to comfort survivors of suicide sometimes inadvertently echo ancient hypothetical arguments for killing oneself. In an online discussion of bad homilies, a writer who goes by the handle Acilius tweeted, "At

Part One. Suicide, Sin, and Grace

the funeral for a cousin of my wife's who had killed himself, the preacher gave a 100% happy-talk sermon about how he was in a better place now. By the end, everyone there was shaken by the clear implication that we should all go and do likewise."[8]

Despite lingering, if inadvertent, echoes of pagan support for suicide in contemporary society, you may have noticed a fundamental difference in the ancient arguments I have outlined so far, and common understandings of suicide today. Both the Stoic-influenced argument for suicide and arguments about women choosing martyrdom over assault assumed that anyone considering suicide was a rational actor weighing the relative merits and ethical implications of various courses of action. Augustine responded to those arguments in kind, meeting their logical propositions with his own, although his were grounded in his faith in God's life-giving love and his awe of God's sovereignty. Today, however, we realize that people who die by suicide are typically in great emotional distress, very often have a diagnosable mental illness, and are not necessarily rational at the moment of their death.

And yet, some of Augustine's insights into suicidality resonate today. He knew, just as you and I do, that "unbearable troubles," as he put it, could drive someone to desire death.[9] But in such a case, Augustine knew, "the will's desire for death is not a desire for nonexistence but a desire for peace."[10] This is commonly acknowledged in suicide intervention today. The person who contemplates suicide doesn't necessarily long for death, as such. Rather, they are desperate for their pain to end, or desperately tired of trying to end it by other means that have not worked.

As a bishop, Augustine sought to offer pastoral instruction to priests and compassionate care to laypersons, while sketching out the boundaries of Christian faith and action in a society suf-

Augustine and Thomas

fused with pagan symbols and values. His strong prohibition of suicide is sometimes misunderstood as him presuming to pass judgment on other people. But his concern for survivors of sexual assault, and his understanding that people seeking suicide were often simply seeking peace, were as pastorally astute as anything the church has ever offered. And as a bishop, his focus was to instruct Christians in how to make a countercultural witness by trusting radically in God, who is revealed in Jesus Christ and is Creator and Lord of everything and everyone. His concerns remain ours.

Christian theologians wrote relatively little about suicide for almost a thousand years after Augustine. The subject appears here and there in law codes and manuals for priests, which typically outlined the rules for withholding the usual burial rites and consigning the corpse to unhallowed ground. Little may have been said about suicide because Christians generally agreed on its meaning and how to deal with it; or because those who disagreed knew it wasn't safe to openly contest orthodoxy, and so kept their thoughts to themselves. Both may well have been true, to varying extents in various places and times.

In the thirteenth century, Thomas Aquinas codified Christian thinking about suicide. He is the theologian most closely identified with my grandmother's belief in suicide as a guaranteed ticket to hell. Drawing on the pagan Greek philosopher Aristotle as well as on Augustine, Thomas argued that human reason can discern some theological truths by observing the world, but that we need faith to show us what reason cannot. His comprehensive work the *Summa Theologiae* was intended to provide a clear overview of Christian doctrine in question-and-answer form.

Part One. Suicide, Sin, and Grace

Question 64, article 5 of the *Summa* deals with suicide.[11] Thomas agreed with Augustine that the commandment against killing prohibits suicide. He went beyond Augustine, however, in presenting three further reasons why suicide is prohibited: it goes against our natural inclination to live; it violates human community; and it rejects God's gift of life.

First, it was self-evident to Thomas not only "that every thing loves itself" but also that every creature has a duty to love itself, meaning, to treat itself well. "Hence," he argued, "self-killing is always a moral sin, inasmuch as it stands against natural law and charity." Second, nothing that exists, exists on its own; it always "belongs to a whole." "Therefore," he continued, drawing on Aristotle's *Ethics*, "he who kills himself injures the community." Finally, because life is God's gift, anyone who dies by suicide "sins against God" by usurping a power that rightfully belongs to God. Citing Deuteronomy 32:39, "I kill and I make alive," Thomas reminded his readers that "to God alone belongs the power over death and life."

Anyone who has ever been depressed might quibble with Thomas's assertions that "every thing loves itself" and that life is a gift. It's a cliché for suicidal people to say their loved ones would be better off without them, but it's a cliché because, almost without exception, they actually believe it. My mother said it to my twelve-year-old self, and nothing I sobbed in my desperate attempts to convince her otherwise could drown out the lies that depression relentlessly repeated inside her own mind.

Thomas's beloved "natural law" doesn't seem like a reliable source when something has gone so terribly awry with nature. And anyone who has been suicidal might reply that in the moment, death seemed like a more valuable gift from God than life. Survivors of suicide attempts have testified to this. One, called

Karen, remembered, "I just wanted not to have this body. I didn't want to continue being in it. I wanted to get free of it. I wanted just to kill that thing and the reality it contained, and I didn't see any other way to do that other than to kill me." Another, Maddie, spoke to her reflection in the bathroom mirror: "I felt completely numb, and I looked at her and said, 'Don't worry, you'll be out of your misery pretty soon.' I just wanted to stop the feelings that I couldn't tolerate, and I couldn't stop them any other way."[12]

Depressed persons may find it impossible to see themselves as lovable or their lives as a gift. That God loves us, and that only God has the right to end our lives, however, are classic tenets of Christian faith. So is the belief that, as baptized members of Jesus Christ's body, we are members of each other; and as members of society, our well-being is wrapped up in the well-being of others. Because we are so interconnected, the harm we do to ourselves reverberates far beyond the self, even when one's goal is to end one's own suffering. Part of the harm that suicide does is to the web of interdependent relationships in which we all live. A suicidal person's pain may keep them from taking any of this to heart, but the church must continue to proclaim it. As John Donne, who struggled with suicidal urges, wrote, "Any man's death diminishes me, because I am involved in mankind."[13]

When it comes to suicide, Thomas Aquinas is probably best remembered for labeling it "the most dangerous" offense because, as he wrote, "there remains no time to expiate the sin through penance." He was not the first to point to the particular spiritual danger inherent in suicide, that unlike other mortal sins such as adultery, suicide by definition could not be confessed and atoned for on this side of the veil. Augustine had written of Judas that "in a fit of self-destructive remorse [he] left himself no chance of a saving repentance."[14]

Part One. Suicide, Sin, and Grace

But what many people now forget is that Thomas, much like Augustine, made this argument not in a vacuum, but rather, to address a specific pastoral problem. Thomas's particular concern was that Christians might kill themselves out of grief or shame for having committed some other wrong, like adultery or even homicide. Thomas wanted Christians to remember that such self-punishment is not God's will for us, nor is it appropriate for human beings to act as our own judge, jury, and executioner.

Sadly, in his desire to turn people away from suicide, Thomas reiterated an argument made by both Aristotle in his *Ethics* and Augustine in *City of God*: that what he called "the appearance of fortitude" in suicide "is not real fortitude, it is some weakness in a soul not strong enough to bear hardship." This impulse to shame still echoes in comments about the "cowardice" or "weakness" of people who kill themselves. These statements can be not only an unfair judgment of the deceased person but also a further source of pain for their family and friends.

The voices of Augustine and Thomas still ring through Christian discussions of suicide. The next chapter will show, however, that their views were not left uncontested, and also that their ideas had consequences that would have horrified both theologians.

CHAPTER FOUR

Unforeseen Consequences

In Dante's epic *Divine Comedy*, people who kill themselves are condemned to the seventh circle of hell. That's the circle reserved for the souls who are guilty of violence. Among murderers and military conquerors like Attila the Hun and Alexander the Great "who gave their hands to blood and plunder," Dante portrays the souls of suicides in a unique way. Because they have robbed their own bodies of life, after death they remain separated from those bodies. Their souls are doomed to pass eternity encased in trees that are gathered together into a wooded area.[1]

The soundscape of Dante's Wood of the Suicides is filled with flapping wings and tortured cries. Swooping, fierce-clawed harpies snatch leaves and snap twigs off the tormented souls' branches in assaults that leave the trees wailing and bleeding. But these wounds are perversely welcome, because within the logic of Dante's cosmos, the trees can only speak while their sap-blood is flowing. The harpies' assaults are these souls' only opportunities to scream out the distress that led them to end their lives. Their final act of communication, in life, had been to do violence to themselves. Now, in a poetic twist, violence inflicted upon them offers their only opportunities to communicate.

Part One. Suicide, Sin, and Grace

In the face of such raw pain that is doomed to endure through eternity, the poet finds no words. The only comfort he can conjure is to gather up the stray leaves that have blown off the branches of a damned tree that was once an acquaintance and place them gently at the base of his trunk. It's a futile but kind gesture, trying to restore some semblance of wholeness to a fellow Christian who tore his own body and soul asunder.

Christians have not left the punishment of suicides solely in God's hands. Earthly penalties have included mutilation of the corpse; denial of the full, or sometimes any, Christian funeral rite; burial not just in unhallowed ground but often in garbage pits; and confiscation of the deceased's property. Writing in response to a question from missionaries to Bulgaria about what to do in cases of suicide, Pope Nicholas I in 866 forbade offering Mass for the repose of the soul who had died in this way. The pope was in good company. Around the same time, high clerics such as the archbishop of Tours and councils of bishops instructed the clergy under their authority not to say funeral Masses for suicides, nor to offer psalms and prayers for them.[2] Variants of such prohibitions continued into the twentieth century; it was 1993 before the Catholic Church's catechism reversed the official teaching that suicide was always a mortal sin.[3]

Two things should be noted, so as not to overstate the church's condemnation of suicide. First, the ninth-century missionaries to Bulgaria would not likely have posed their question to the pope had they considered the matter settled. They might not have had much experience with known suicides (as opposed to deaths that could have been accidental). But regardless of how often they encountered suicide, they may have hoped for

Unforeseen Consequences

a response offering them some pastoral leeway. And perhaps, when they didn't receive that leeway, they simply took it. We can't know. Second, people who died by suicide were not the only ones to be denied a full Christian burial. People executed for crimes; people "who put themselves to death by any form of negligence whatever," in the words of the archbishop of Tours; and people who were killed in duels were, at the time, all to be treated in the same way as those who deliberately caused their own death. For Pope Nicholas, at least, deterrence was a strong motivation for denying the normal rites; he hoped, as he wrote, "that fear may be struck into other people."[4] Not all the penalties enacted upon suicides were particular to them; they were not all designed for retribution or condemnation of the deceased; and they were not always known or accepted by all the clergy who were supposed to carry them out. Ambivalence, hesitancy, and compassion seem always to have played a role in the treatment of suicide, even at times when canon law was explicit.

This tension between law and practice appears in Shakespeare's *Hamlet*, written at the turn of the seventeenth century. Two men debate the law as they dig a grave for Ophelia, who has drowned herself. When one affirms that Ophelia is to have a Christian burial, his colleague asks, "How can that be, unless she drowned herself in her own defense?" (Self-defense being the principal Christian justification for homicide.) The other concedes that Ophelia's class position played a part, saying, "If this had not been a gentlewoman, she should have been buried out o' Christian burial." A little later, when Ophelia's brother Laertes notes with surprise the brevity of his sister's rite, the officiating priest counters, "Her obsequies have been as far enlarged as we have warranties . . . we should profane the service of the dead to sing a requiem and such rest to her as to peace-parted souls." The

43

Part One. Suicide, Sin, and Grace

priest believes he's being charitable, but Laertes has a different perspective on his sister's ultimate fate. He flings at the cleric: "I tell thee, churlish priest, a ministering angel shall my sister be, when thou liest howling."[5]

For much of history, proving a particular death a suicide was almost impossible, except in the most obvious cases. At times and in places where most people couldn't swim, deaths by drowning were easy to rule accidental; accidental poisonings have historically been common as well. Although autopsies have long been performed, they were not routine until relatively recently. Illiterate people couldn't leave notes, and the literate had a strong incentive not to, given the stakes. Anyone considering suicide had options available to preserve deniability.

As we have already seen, there have always been clergy who took a relatively nuanced pastoral approach to suicide, recognizing the need to affirm the value of each person's life and also the terrible burden any particular person might have been carrying. Martin Luther recognized this burden in remarking to a group of friends that, when people killed themselves, it was "very certain" that "'tis the devil who has put the cord round their necks, or the knife to their throats." Elaborating on this theme, Luther went on to tell his dinner companions, "I don't share the opinion that suicides are certainly to be damned. My reason is that they do not wish to kill themselves but are overcome by the power of the devil. They are like a man who is murdered in the woods by a robber."[6]

Secular writers about suicide have frequently misunderstood Luther's view of Satan's role in it. Psychologist Kay Redfield Jamison has written that "many theologians [asserted] that suicide was among the more unforgivable of sins—Martin Luther, for example, wrote that suicide was the work of the Devil." Jamison misses the fact that Luther was actually offering compassion for people who kill themselves. In fact, he specifically said he believed they were not necessarily condemned to hell.[7] The corresponding view today would be to recognize, as Dr. Jamison's usually helpful work does, the role mental illness typically plays in suicide.

Luther's vision of the devil luring people to their deaths arose from his own experience of a long physical and mental health crisis starting in his forties. Cardiac-circulatory troubles combined with depression, then called "melancholy," in a vicious circle that, for Luther, constituted an assault by the devil. These physical, mental, and spiritual troubles persisted to varying degrees for two decades until his death.[8] Luther wrote to his friend and fellow Reformed theologian Johannes Agricola, "Satan himself is raging against me with all his might. . . . He affects me with indescribable spiritual weakness. . . . But I know that I have taught the Word of Christ purely and truly for the salvation of many. That is what the Devil is angry at, that is why he wants to crush me together with the Word."[9] Around the same time, he asked his fellow theologian Philip Melanchthon to pray for him, describing himself as a "miserable worm" but stating nonetheless, "I hope that the God who began His work in me will ultimately have mercy on me, for I seek and thirst after nothing but the merciful God."[10]

Despite his own struggles, or perhaps because of them, Luther recognized the potentially life-saving value of moral opprobrium around suicide. His belief that satanic forces were responsible for self-inflicted deaths "ought not," he said, "be taught to the common people." Life in sixteenth-century Europe was so

Part One. Suicide, Sin, and Grace

miserable for so many that Luther feared if his belief were publicized, it would give "Satan . . . an opportunity to cause slaughter." People who died by suicide, and customs like not bringing their corpses into the church for funeral services, served as "examples," Luther said, "by which our Lord God wishes to show that the devil is powerful and also that we should be diligent in prayer. But for these examples, we would not fear God."[11]

Luther cautioned against seeming to approve suicide at a time when the number of recorded crimes—of which suicide was legally one—and recorded accidents was skyrocketing in northern Europe. For example, in southeastern England, historian Alexander Murray notes, more than nine times as many suicides were recorded in 1565 as in 1514. This increase occurred, Murray notes, "against a background of a massive increase in all recorded crime," and of a fifteen-fold increase in verdicts of accidental death. The trend held true in German-speaking states.[12] Centuries later, these legal records leave us with questions. Did suicides and accidents greatly increase in the sixteenth century, or were coroners simply being more assiduous in ferreting them out and recording them? Whether or not the actual increase was as great as records suggest, Luther would likely have been aware of the seemingly growing number of suicides, and leery of playing any role in adding to it.

Thomas Aquinas cannot have foreseen the lengths to which some desperate Christians would take his argument that suicide was the "most dangerous" sin. I suspect he would have been horrified to know that, faced with the prospect of eternal damnation, along with the desecration of their body and the public humiliation of their family, Christians looking for a less-fraught escape from this life sometimes turned to murder instead.

Examples abound. In 1704 in Germany, Agnes Catherina Schickin, a thirty-year-old servant, quietly and deliberately killed a seven-year-old boy and then immediately confessed. When asked why she would target an innocent child, Schickin answered that he was "saved" and was surely in heaven, while her sole motivation for killing him was her desire to "leave the world." As recorded in the notes of her testimony, she trusted she would get her wish, as "the hangman would surely dispatch her."[13] Before execution, she would have the opportunity to confess and be absolved, sparing herself eternal damnation. Schickin's actions followed a pattern that was familiar at the time: she chose a victim who was not yet old enough to have committed a serious sin and would therefore die in a state of grace; and she turned herself in to the authorities before anyone was even aware the child was missing. Historian Kathy Stuart has found 116 documented cases of what she terms "suicide by proxy" committed between 1612 and 1839 in the Holy Roman Empire (which included parts of what are now France, Germany, and Italy).[14] Other historians have noted the phenomenon across a variety of European countries.[15] The perpetrators were men and women, Catholics and Protestants; what they had in common was their desire to die and their dread of hell.

The same combination of suicidal desire and dread has pushed people in other settings to take similar action. In the nineteenth-century penal colonies of Australia, conditions were so abysmal that many prisoners expressed a desire to die. Irish convicted thief Laurence Frayne felt "heartsick of my own existence" but was unable to bring himself to what he called "that climax of human depravity, to take away my own life with my own hands."[16] In the face of their theological and psychological aversion to suicide, prisoners made pacts, which historian Robert

Part One. Suicide, Sin, and Grace

Hughes calls "suicide by lottery." A group of convicts would draw straws to choose two men, one of whom would kill the other. For the two suicidal people, this seemed a mutually beneficial arrangement: one would die immediately, and the other would shortly be executed. The rest of the group served as witnesses in an open-and-shut case.[17] It's impossible to know how often these pacts were made, but several records of them exist.

The phenomena of suicides by proxy and murder-suicide pacts by Christians lead to an obvious conclusion: that people desperate to end their lives have long found ways to do so, despite their fear of eternal damnation. Such lethal creativity in the face of theological obstacles meant to deter suicide reminds anyone with a shred of humility that to opine about Christian ethics can be a perilous venture. A doctrine elaborated with the goal of increasing reverence for human life might well deter some, like my grandmother, but it might lead others to spill more blood, not less. Christians can't remain silent in the face of suicide, but we must speak of it with humility.

CHAPTER FIVE

Sinful Settings

Further complicating the Christian ethics of suicide is this fact: examples abound of people who have killed themselves because of the violence self-professed Christians have inflicted on them. To cite a notorious example, the system of chattel slavery placed untold numbers of people in the position of choosing their own death rather than enduring further dehumanization. Around 1784, a trafficked African man onboard a slave ship used his fingernails to rip open his own throat. Members of the European crew tied his hands in response, but, as the ship's physician Thomas Trotter later testified to the British Parliament, "he still however adhered to his resolution, refused all sustenance, and died in about a week or ten days afterwards of mere want of food." To the member of Parliament who asked Trotter if he thought the enslaved man was insane, the doctor replied, "By no means insane; I believe a degree of delirium might [have] come on before he perished, but at the time when he came on board, I believe that he was perfectly in his senses." As historian Marcus Rediker states, "The man's decision to use his own fingernails to rip open his throat was an entirely rational response to landing on a slave ship."[1]

Such suicides were common among enslaved persons. Some killed themselves while they were being trafficked. They

Part One. Suicide, Sin, and Grace

hanged or strangled themselves, or, while being driven overland, jumped from deadly heights or beat their heads against rocks.[2] Attempted self-starvation occurred so frequently onboard slave ships that captains kept on hand a *speculum oris*, a metal device designed to force and lock open a person's jaw so food could be poured down their throat.

Other captives leaped off slave ships, like two women in the late eighteenth century who plunged over the side folded in each other's arms. This form of escape was common enough that slavers soon learned to install netting on all sides of their ships. Those who managed to evade the nets knew they would drown on the open sea if they were not first torn apart by sharks, and yet European eyewitnesses testified to the joy many escapees appeared to feel. One seaman wrote that a captive gone overboard "went down as if exulting that he got away." Another ship's surgeon noted that an escaped man, who was an experienced swimmer like many coastal Africans, "made signs which it is impossible for me to describe in words, expressive of the happiness he had in escaping from us," although the waves eventually overpowered him.[3]

Most of the people who escaped were not Christian. In fact, as theologian Yolanda Pierce has noted, "many of those who were enslaved first encountered the symbol of the cross flying on the flag of the ship that carried them to enslavement."[4] In the face of such a diabolical use of the cross, West African people marshaled their own spiritual, emotional, and physical resources. In these cases, as Willie James Jennings writes, suicide "was considered 'an admirable act,' a kind of martyrdom, especially for those people who believed that in death they would . . . return home, free and without pain."[5] For this reason, historian William Dillon Piersen refers to these deaths as "one of the world's greatest, but most overlooked, religious martyrdoms."[6]

Sinful Settings

Yet, as Jennings notes, in the context of the slave trade, in which Europeans sought to remake Africans into slaves and themselves into supreme beings, "suicide in this case was more than an option. It was a supreme temptation, a false sign of freedom, and therefore a sign of death's victory. In this temptation the voice of death spoke louder than the signs of life, muffled as they were by the groans coming from the holds."[7] Note that Jennings is not passing judgment on those who killed themselves. He is citing suicide as one of the ways in which, as he writes, "Death revealed itself aboard the slave ship as a power, as an antilife form pressing its way deep into the ecology of slave ship life."[8] Death touched every element of the slave trade, most dramatically for Africans but not only for them. As Jennings points out, 50 percent of the slave-trading sailors who traveled to Africa's west coast died there.[9]

In a context in which white people sought to harness the power of violence and death to dehumanize Black people (while unintentionally dehumanizing themselves), it was not only the recently enslaved who might prefer death. The memoirs of self-liberated African Americans recount many suicides. In 1857, Austin Steward told the story of a man who, faced with recapture, "rightly thought death was far preferable" and slit his own throat.[10] As Charles Ball meditated on the thoughts of hanging himself that he had entertained after being sold away to South Carolina from his wife and children in Maryland, he recalled, "It appeared to me that such an act, done by a man in my situation, could not be a violation of the precepts of religion, nor of the laws of God."[11]

Some enslaved persons sought more passive paths to death. Solomon Northup wrote of a woman named Patsey, who offered him bribes to kill and bury her secretly. Although he declined her

Part One. Suicide, Sin, and Grace

request, as he later reflected on the merciless beatings Patsey withstood, Northup came to the conclusion that her death would have been "blessed."[12] Similarly, the sexual and other physical abuse Harriet Jacobs suffered led her to pray repeatedly for death. Sometimes after a beating, as she wrote in her memoir, she "begged" her friends to let her die, "rather than send for the doctor."[13]

Suicide is connected to the belief that at least some Africans, and their American descendants, could fly. At least some American stories about that ability are connected to a mass suicide, or mass flight, in 1803. In the spring of that year, a group of enslaved Igbo people from what is now Nigeria, bound for St. Simon's Island, Georgia, revolted just off the island's coast, forcing the white crew into the water to drown. When the ship they had commandeered ran aground, the Igbo people themselves walked into the marsh, east toward their homeland. They either drowned in the process or, as local resident Wallace Quarterman recalled in the 1930s, "rose up in the sky and turned themselves into buzzards and flew right back to Africa."[14] The spot where they entered the water has since been known as Ebos Landing (using an alternate spelling of Igbo).[15] The memory of these and other ancestors survived through generations of testimony about "folks what could fly back to Africa," as one formerly enslaved man recalled, emphasizing, "They could take wing and just fly off."[16]

Belief in the phenomenon of flying Africans also integrated instances of self-liberation when enslaved persons "flew off" to free states or Canada. Where the line sits between actual and metaphorical flight in these accounts is not for me to say. I accept that at least some, if not all, of these stories may tell of actual flight. As a Christian, and as a person influenced by the pre-Christian beliefs of my Scottish ancestors, I believe many things that are at least as strange, if not more so. Nobel Prize–winning author Toni Morrison once commented, "The one thing you say about a myth is that there's some truth in there, no matter how bizarre they may seem." Noting that the Works Progress Administration interviewers who collected the memories of elderly Black Americans in the 1930s routinely asked whether their interlocutors had ever heard of flying Africans, Morrison said they received one of two answers. Either the respondents said, "No, I never saw it, but I heard about it," or, in Morrison's words, "they said they *had* seen it." Most tellingly, Morrison noted, "No one said, 'What are you talking about?' They all had heard of it."[17] In a context in which the law, the economy, the church, most of what white society accepted as science, and the vast majority of white people denied enslaved people's humanity, selfhood, and right to move freely, the ability to fly could signify actual flight, or Black people gathering to worship or celebrate, slipping away at night to visit family or a lover down the road, escaping to legal freedom across a border, finding joy in a myriad of ways—or choosing death.

In her novel *Song of Solomon*, Morrison conveys the cost one person's flight can exact from their family or community. The novel tells of an enslaved man, Solomon, who disappeared one day, leaving a wife and twenty-one children. Solomon didn't run away, the narrator says. "He flew. You know, like a bird. Just stood up in the fields one day, ran up some hill, spun around a couple of times, and was lifted up in the air." His wife, the story went, "screamed out loud for days." People said she screamed out of love, as (commentators believed) women were prone to do when they lost their man. But the narrator muses, "I always thought it was trying to take care of children by themselves, you know what I mean?"[18] Spouses left widowed, children left orphaned, a co-parent's support gone; scars of loss left not only on a family but

Part One. Suicide, Sin, and Grace

also on their community for generations: these are reminders of the violent legacy of suicide, itself in many cases a response to unfathomable systemic violence.

A person who carries out the decision to end their own life always does so in a particular context. And very often, that context does not support the person's thriving, and may contribute to their despair and their feeling of being trapped. The examples are myriad.

American suicide rates declined between 2018 and 2020, and then rose again in 2021. Did the COVID-19 pandemic and social isolation play a role?

American Indians and Alaska Natives have the country's highest rate of suicide at 28.1 instances per 100,000 people.[19] Indigenous journalist Tanya Talaga has noted that suicide among indigenous people worldwide is a modern phenomenon, dating from the last few generations.[20] Their suicides seem clearly connected with ongoing genocide, which Australian Aboriginal psychiatrist Helen Milroy describes as "wanting to remove us from the Earth permanently," and which is "trauma on a more massive scale" than even the intergenerational trauma whose effects we still seek to understand.[21]

When we consider Americans' race and sex together, we see it's white men who most frequently kill themselves, at a rate of 25.23 per 100,000, followed by American Indian men at 24.81 per 100,000.[22] The fact that men are likely to use firearms to kill themselves contributes to their high rates of completed suicide. But the statistics raise a question: Do white racism and sexism also take a toll on those who benefit from them?

Suicide statistics don't typically include information about sexuality or about gender beyond the male-female binary. A 2021 survey of thirty-five thousand LGBTQ people between the ages of thirteen and twenty-four, however, found that 42 percent had seriously considered attempting suicide in the past year, including more than half of transgender and nonbinary youth. Ninety-four percent of them agreed "that recent politics negatively impacted their mental health." Further, the survey found that "more than 80% of LGBTQ youth stated that COVID-19 made their living situation more stressful—and only 1 in 3 LGBTQ youth found their home to be LGBTQ-affirming."[23]

Over the past couple of decades, rates of suicide among Black children, adolescents, and young adults have been growing much faster than those among their white and Latino counterparts. Research has shown that racial discrimination contributes to suicidality. It's also likely that Black young people needing mental health care are, instead, defined as having behavioral problems and punished rather than supported.[24]

Finally, the age group of eighty-five and older is most at risk of killing themselves—and also experience significant isolation, depression, and other health troubles.[25]

Patterns like these lead thoughtful people to wonder how social and economic conditions, history, cultural resources, and community bonds may make suicide more or less likely for any person. You and I may be appropriately horrified, for example, when we read that seventeenth-century Anglicans built a church on top of a slave dungeon they controlled in Ghana. As Episcopal lay minister Annette Buchanan says, "While the enslaved people were beneath crying out in agony, starving, [Anglicans] were having a church service."[26] As we wrestle with history, it's important to ask a follow-up question: Where might we still be harnessing the Christian faith to murderous systems, contributing to the deaths of our fellow children of God?

Part One. Suicide, Sin, and Grace

Context matters. It matters when we consider social and cultural factors and the identities of people at risk for suicide, and it matters when we think about depression, substance use disorders, and bipolar disorder, the mental illnesses most closely associated with suicide.[27] Journalist Johann Hari makes this point when he notes that current mental health research indicates that "the genetic factors that contribute to depression and anxiety are very real, but they also need a trigger in your environment or your psychology. Your genes can then supercharge those factors, but they can't create them alone."[28] Rejecting binary thinking about depression as either purely "a moral failing" or simply "a brain disease" is by no means original to Hari.[29] The World Health Organization has long defined the determinants of mental health as "a complex interplay of individual, social and structural stresses and vulnerabilities."[30] To me, this bio-psycho-social model of understanding mental distress makes sense: taking into account the wide range of genetic, social, economic, and cultural factors and personal experiences that might cause mental illness and then suicidality. The church can work to improve social and economic conditions that can contribute to mental illness and suicidality, and also offer support to people at risk of killing themselves.

It is true that people kill themselves in (what seem to others as) far less dire circumstances than chattel slavery. Often, we can't know why they did so, or why, in contrast, someone in a similar—or arguably worse—situation never becomes suicidal. As Christians, what we can do is be frank and say that suicide is a reality in this fallen world. It exists, it's out there, and people will think about it and do it. If you're not thinking about suicide, wondering whether life (or your life in particular) is worth living, someone around you is. Someone, even, in your church. To say that suicide is an enduring human problem—what Albert Camus famously called the "one truly serious philosophical problem"—is not to say that Christians should accept it.[31] It's to say that we should expect it. And we are called to witness to the enduring possibilities of life, and to stand with those tempted to end it and most closely affected by such temptation.

PART TWO

The Communion of Saints

CHAPTER SIX

The Suicidal Christian

One of my favorite Bible passages is one of the bleakest.

"O Lord, I cry to you for help; in the morning my prayer comes before you. Lord, why have you rejected me? Why have you hidden your face from me?"[1] The Eighty-Eighth Psalm is unique among the psalms of lament in expressing utter despair from its opening to its closing verse: "My friend and my neighbor you have put away from me, and darkness is my only companion."[2]

My experience with suicide is what makes Psalm 88 so comforting to me. This desperate prayer gives voice to the pain that leads so many people to suicide. Its inclusion in the Psalter tells me that there is a place for deep despair, and for those wracked by it, in the prayers and communities of the faithful. This inclusion is an ancient affirmation by Jewish and Christian believers that God hears, sees, and loves us when our emotional landscape is so arid we can't believe God could possibly abide there with us. If this psalm or one very like it didn't exist, I believe Scripture would be lacking.[3]

And yet, I wouldn't expect this psalm to comfort someone in an actively depressed or suicidal state. In fact, these verses of Scripture would make an expressive suicide note.

Part Two. *The Communion of Saints*

Kathryn Greene-McCreight has described her dilemma as an Episcopal priest, a theologian, and a person who lives with bipolar disorder and has had suicidal thoughts. "How," she asks, "could I confess my faith in the God who is 'a very present help in trouble' (Psalm 46:1) when I felt entirely abandoned by that God?"[4] One could answer that Psalm 46 can be a prayer for God's help, asking God to be present so that those praying might "not fear, though the earth be moved." And the person who feels "entirely abandoned" might retort that only someone who did not feel so deeply, miserably alone could take that perspective.

Greene-McCreight goes on to point out that mental illness makes it difficult, if not impossible, to do what the Westminster Catechism and other confessions of faith agree is the purpose of the Christian life: to glorify and enjoy God forever.[5] Why, she has wondered, if she is a Christian, is she not filled with joy?[6] When I read my fellow priest's pained questions, I want to reassure her that God adores her as she is. And yet, I see her point. If joy and peace are acknowledged in Scripture as fruits of the Spirit, does that mean the Spirit is not at work in a depressed or suicidal person?[7] Of course it doesn't: the list of the fruits of the Spirit is not a checklist we must complete to prove to ourselves or to God that we are worthy of God's love. God, who consistently takes the side of those who are suffering, deeply loves people who live with mental illness.

For the suicidal person, however, it's easy to see the fruits of the Spirit as just one more list of one's personal failings. A commonly noted feature of the suicidal mind is tunnel vision. The person's psychic pain is so intense that their attention is drawn to it more and more exclusively. This focused state leaves no room for other thoughts, options, recourses. As Greene-McCreight writes, "When I am depressed, it seems that the only way not to hurt is to cease being a center of consciousness . . . when I am [depressed], there is no 'other side,' no perspective, no reminding myself that this will pass . . . yes, of course I remind myself of this, but it only enters the top of my brain and then flits right out again."[8]

The experiences of other suicidal Christians echo Greene-McCreight's. Quaker writer Parker Palmer has said, "In depression, God is dead, or so it was for me. As a result, I can't write warmly about how 'God was with me every step of the way,' helping me survive depression and thrive on the other side." Palmer did survive and thrive, and thus has what he calls "personal knowledge of resurrection."[9] But holding on long enough to survive and thrive takes energy that many people, struggling with mental illness, losses, or various kinds of violence directed toward them, simply don't have. Palmer knows this. He writes, "I understand why some depressed people kill themselves: they need the rest."[10] Gillian Marchenko, an evangelical Christian, testifies to this fatigue. She describes her thoughts in the grip of depression: "'Please God, take this [depression] away,' I pray when I can. . . . My thoughts muddy. I shiver. I sleep for hours and wake up exhausted. Always exhausted. No amount of sleep reenergizes me."[11]

I know my mother would affirm the unquenchable need for rest to which Palmer and Marchenko testify. She did so in her last written communication. "I simply can't go on," she wrote in the note she left on her kitchen table the night she died. "I am simply too tired to fight my way back."

Although Christians may keep our experiences of mental illness to ourselves, our faith does not make us immune to these disorders. A 2022 survey of Protestant pastors in the United States found that 54 percent had known at least one congregant diagnosed with a significant mental illness like clinical depression, bipolar disorder, or schizophrenia. Twenty-six percent of respondents acknowledged having personally experienced a mental illness. That proportion rose to 37 percent of pastors under forty-five, possibly suggesting that younger pastors are more likely to acknowledge mental illness or to seek a diagnosis, or both.[12]

Six in ten pastoral respondents said they broached the topic of mental illness in a sermon or other large group address at least once a year, while 37 percent said they rarely or never brought it up (down from 49 percent in a similar survey in 2014). Over 80 percent said they offered some sort of support for people with mental illness, from therapist referral lists to support for families or offering space to community support groups.[13]

Surveys like these don't offer any information about the helpfulness or unhelpfulness of pastors' conceptions of mental illness, or of the resources they offer. Christians who suffer from depression, the mental illness most strongly correlated with suicide, are often faced with distinctively unhelpful explanations of their disease—bad theology that can be harmful to boot. Christian psychologists often frame depression as a lack of gratitude, rebellion against God, or denial of the resurrection. In these views, theologian Jessica Coblentz notes, "The presumption is that good Christians harness their freedom to choose to be happy and thankful, while sinners choose to dwell in depression."[14] Coblentz cites the example of comedian Steve Harvey, who credits his habit of starting the day with "gratitude prayer" for his lack of depression. "You cannot be depressed and grateful at the same time," Harvey says. "So, I remove all depression and I start my whole day with gratitude."[15] As Coblentz points out, these Christians assume that one's "affective experience of the world" is entirely within one's control.[16] As a person who has experienced clinical depression, I can testify that it is not. Depression, for me, is like a miasma that seeps into my mind, body, and soul, fouling everything it touches even before I have had a chance to notice how far it has spread. Framing that harmful occupation against my will as a failure to practice gratitude—as, implicitly, a sin on my part—is insulting, however helpful Harvey may find it for himself.

Also problematic, I think, is the tendency to present depression, in Coblentz's words, "as a form of divine instruction" that, "while trying, is ultimately gifted by God for the sake of advancing personal holiness."[17] Kathryn Greene-McCreight takes this approach in her theological meditation on mental illness and her own experience of bipolar disorder. Greene-McCreight affirms that "mental illness is not an indication of the weakness of one's faith." She goes on, however, to say that "it may be ... a test and should be met like all other tests: with prayer that God will see us through it faithfully, that we will be seen faithful, and that we should be found at the last without reproach, that God will use it to our benefit and us to his glory."[18]

As a survivor of parental suicide, and as a person who has lived long enough to see grace abound in a multitude of sinful situations, I believe both that God walks with us in pain and tragedy and that God is always working to bring whatever good might be possible out of those situations. I don't believe, however, that mental illness is ever a test imposed by God. That being said, if I encountered a Christian who did believe that, and if this framework were helpful to them, I would assure them that they were not meant to meet the test alone. I would encourage them to identify and ask for what they needed from their church to help them emerge victorious—and alive.

Part Two. The Communion of Saints

The cofounder of the Catholic Worker movement, Dorothy Day, was known for attending Mass daily and devoting hours of each overfilled day to personal prayer. Among the people for whom Dorothy prayed were friends and acquaintances who had died by suicide. A traditional Catholic, born just before the turn of the twentieth century, Dorothy accepted the church's teaching that suicide was a mortal sin. She refused, however, to accept that doctrine could tie God's hands. As her biographer Jim Forest states, "She prayed that those who had taken their own lives would have the grace of final repentance. That her prayers occurred long after their deaths was of no matter, she said, 'because there is no time with God.'"[19] People who died by suicide were not the only supposedly lost souls for whom Dorothy prayed. In a 1948 article insisting on the possibility of salvation for committed atheists, Dorothy wrote, "Dear God, may Lenin too find a place of refreshment, light and peace. Or don't we believe in retroactive prayers? There is no time with God."[20]

Dorothy Day's compassion for people tempted to suicide arose at least in part from her own experience. She had known suicidal despair after the loss of love affairs, and in the wake of an illegal abortion and its associated health complications. In a 1973 letter to a young woman in crisis, Dorothy wrote, "I'm praying very hard for you this morning, because I myself have been through much of what you have been through. Twice I tried to take my own life, and the dear Lord pulled me thru [*sic*] that darkness—I was rescued from that darkness."[21]

Dorothy Day died in 1980, just a few years too early to see the Catholic Church's Code of Canon Law revised to allow full funeral rites, with burial in consecrated ground, for people who died by suicide. By the early 1990s, the church's catechism taught as doctrine the practice that Dorothy had undertaken decades before. It now states, "We should not despair of the eternal salvation of persons who have taken their own lives. By ways known to him alone, God can provide the opportunity for salutary repentance. The Church prays for persons who have taken their own lives."[22]

I think it's important to acknowledge that we don't, in fact, know that people who have killed themselves didn't repent of their actions in their final moments, when it was too late to prevent their death. Some survivors of suicide attempts have said they felt deep dismay at the point when it was too late to turn back. Ken Baldwin is one such survivor, one of only a tiny percentage to survive leaping off San Francisco's Golden Gate Bridge. As soon as he went over the railing, he later told a journalist, he realized, "Everything in my life that I thought was unfixable was totally fixable, except for having just jumped." When he saw his hands leave the bridge, Baldwin said, he "realized what a stupid thing I was doing. And there was nothing I could do but fall." According to journalist John Bateson, "He thought of his young family, and suddenly wanted to live."[23]

Wanting to live, wishing to turn back toward life: that sounds like repentance to me.

When Ken Baldwin speaks of his suicide attempt, and realizing that all his problems were actually fixable except for having jumped off the Golden Gate Bridge, he is—to state the obvious—narrating his experience in retrospect. In the moment before he went over the railing, leaping seemed like his only option. That conviction is the primary characteristic of the suicidal mind in Western-oriented societies and persons, and possibly others; but it's likely not the case for everyone.

Edwin Shneidman, a psychologist and leader in the study of suicidality, showed through his extensive research that people in a suicidal crisis have a tightly constricted emotional and intellectual perception of themselves and their circumstances. "There was nothing else to do"; "The only way out was death"; of these beliefs Shneidman wrote, "These are examples of the constricted mind at work."[24] If a listener is paying attention, this constriction can be noticed in the potentially suicidal person's use of words indicating they are trapped in an all-or-nothing perspective. Those words can be terribly simple. As Shneidman affirmed, "The single most dangerous word in all of suicidology is the four-letter word *only*."[25]

Because of this constriction, suicidally depressed people often don't have a sense of a future self. To the extent that depression perpetuates the assumption that nothing will ever get better, a depressed person may stay stuck in, as Jessica Coblentz describes it, "a prison of the present—a hell-on-earth; an eternal, unfamiliar, inhospitable landscape."[26] If they see that experience as permanent—or perhaps, as my mother did, as something she was "simply too tired to fight"—they are at risk for suicide.

Everything I have said here may be true for any particular suicidal person, and it is true for vast numbers of suicidal people; these patterns have been carefully observed. It's important to note, however, that these patterns are also culturally constructed and reflect a Western mind-set. Anthropologist Lisa Stevenson's work with Inuit people in Canada showed her the need for humility in cross-cultural work regarding suicide. She believes there is value in taking people seriously when they say they will be better off dead. In the face of genocidal colonial policies, she notes, "it may be that any hope one has lies beyond life itself."[27] Through her

The Suicidal Christian

encounters with young Inuit people, Stevenson learned, "If listening to the pain in the lives of suicidal youth is only a means to the end of keeping Inuit youth alive, one ceases to hear much of anything. Listening—when life is radically in question—meant taking very seriously uncertainty about life and death."[28]

Depending on the cultural context, suicide may not always represent the closing off of imaginative possibilities. Stevenson raises the possibility that not everyone develops the tunnel vision so often noted by Western researchers and mental health practitioners.[29] In fact, it may be colonizing forces that have tunnel vision with regard to indigenous people (or others who are dispossessed or marginalized). Stevenson asks, "Do we [i.e., colonizers], in our policies, programs, and exhortations, ask Inuit to live while also expecting them to die?"[30]

Stevenson's work is a reminder to listen to suicidal people—from all backgrounds—as they narrate their own experiences, feelings, and beliefs. What one hears might be disturbing, but it's crucial to listen with open minds and hearts, setting aside one's own desire to be "successful" in "helping" the suicidal person. Where possible, this listening should be offered by someone of the same group—at least in cases where significant power dynamics are in play. If that's not possible, and if the person offering support is from a dominant or privileged group, the supporter needs to take extra care to exercise humility. This is an appropriate acknowledgment, not only of the diversity of God's people but also of the power dynamics that persist through genocides perpetrated with the church's blessing.

When a Christian is in the grip of suicidal thoughts, it's the role of their faith community to understand their perspective while

Part Two. The Communion of Saints

also offering a different point of view. We can accompany them without blaming or shaming them; without decrying their supposedly inadequate faith; without misreading their psychic pain as a marker of a particularly sinful soul. We can act on the understanding that they are one of God's beloved, who is experiencing a searingly acute form of the pain of inhabiting a creation that groans while awaiting its full liberation from the power of death.[31] And yet, this creation has also already been transformed by Jesus Christ's resurrection. The suicidal person is constrained from trusting in the reality of the resurrection—as we all are, from time to time. But Christian communities can channel our trust in the resurrection to equip us to accompany God's people who are in suicidal distress. Together, we can embody our conviction that God has not forgotten them, by showing that we have not.

In James Baldwin's *Another Country*, Rufus remains in relationship with God even as he hurtles toward death. Rufus's final words, as he's leaping off the George Washington Bridge, are, "All right, you motherfucking Godalmighty bastard, I'm coming to you." Theologian and literary scholar Tiffany Eberle Kriner characterizes those last words as, "As profound a confession of faith as I have ever heard."[32] A child of the church, Rufus knows there is nowhere to flee from God. Even as he flings himself toward his Creator, he's still a member of the communion of saints.

CHAPTER SEVEN

Suicide and the Communion of Saints

"Do not harm yourself, for we are all here." That's what Paul shouts to his jailer in Philippi to keep the man from killing himself, in the sixteenth chapter of Acts. The jailer had slept through the earthquake that shook the prison's foundations and caused its inmates' chains to fall off. Not wanting the guard to come to any harm, whether by a superior or self-inflicted, Paul and Silas had stuck around the prison. Now, seeing the man draw his sword to kill himself, Paul calls out. The guard is so moved by this inconceivable turn of events that he gets baptized along with his entire family, committing his household to follow the Way of Jesus.

What happened for that prison guard would ideally be the case for every person considering suicide: a caring community calling out, "Do not harm yourself, for we are with you," and backing up that reassurance with loving presence.

Christianity professes not only that our stories are intertwined, but that our very selves are, too. Paul used the metaphor of Christ's body to teach this point: that baptism unites us in Jesus and makes us mutually available to and dependent upon each other. Christians are called to tend to each other's spiritual, emotional, and physical well-being, and to offer God's loving care to people outside the church as well. Otherwise, the New Testament would not include so many exhortations to "Rejoice with those who rejoice, weep with those who weep" (Rom. 12:15), "Bear one another's burdens" (Gal. 6:2), and share food and clothing with neighbors who have less (such as 1 Cor. 11:21–22; James 2:15–16). Even Paul's reassurance that "[God] will not let you be tested beyond your strength" (1 Cor. 10:13) is addressed to the whole congregation—to "y'all" in southern English, or "ustedes" in American Spanish—not to one person.

Our connection in Christ extends across time and space in the communion of saints. The Episcopal Church's Book of Common Prayer defines this communion as "the whole family of God, the living and the dead, those whom we love and those whom we hurt, bound together in Christ by sacrament, prayer, and praise."[1]

In cases of suicide, love and hurt are closely intertwined. People experiencing suicidal thoughts often find it impossible to believe anyone truly loves them. Usually, they are convinced that those they leave behind will be better off without them. And when they die, the complicated feelings of those they leave behind reflect both love and hurt.

The church's teachings about suicide, and the long-standing assumption of many Christians that people who died by suicide were consigned to hell, have made those feelings more complicated, and arguably more painful. Catholic theologian Elizabeth Antus has argued that precisely because of those past teachings, "it is crucial" to include people who die by suicide "completely within the communion of saints" as "an act of hospitality that entails praying for and with suicide decedents and believing in hope that they live now in God's embrace."[2] As heirs of harmful church teachings, we have a responsibility to offer more hopeful perspectives that more fully express our trust in God's grace. We can strive to be a community that not only remembers before God people who have taken their own lives but also offers compassionate support to their survivors and to people in danger of dying by suicide, of any faith and of no faith at all. We can move from "Don't kill yourself or you'll go to hell," beyond "Don't worry, your loved one isn't in hell," to "Do not harm yourself, for we are all here"—and we will stay with you.

I wrote earlier that the belief that people who die by suicide are condemned to hell may have helped my grandmother stay alive. I do think that's true. What I also believe to be true, however, is that a more merciful theology in a more equitable society would have helped her immeasurably more, facilitating not only her survival but also her thriving. If her hardworking but economically poor father had had appropriate social support, he might have been able to keep his children at home after his wife's death. Instead, in a turn of events that is familiar to many people today, the local government saw his poverty as a sign of his unfitness to parent and placed his children in foster care hundreds of miles away. As they grew up in a culture that made no room for them to express their pain at the far-too-early loss of their mother, and to incorporate a sense of their mother's presence—not just her tragic, unspeakable absence—in their lives, my grandmother and her four siblings learned that their mother's story was too shameful to be told. And both theology and politics were complicit in their pain being passed down.

Only one person has ever been astute enough—and direct enough—to ask me if I miss my mother. She intuited what my answer would be: I don't. My mother had been dead twenty-five years before something happened that made me think I'd like to be able to call and tell her about it—a childhood friend of mine died, a friend my mother had liked and about whom she had worried. Am I grateful for the gifts my mother gave me, like the ability to delight in a crisp salad, creamy milk chocolate, and the whir of a hummingbird's wings? Deeply. Do I think the world is better off without her? Not at all. She was generous, loved to laugh, and grew beautiful flowers. Her death diminished her communities. Do I lament her death? Absolutely. It breaks my heart that she died as she did, at the age of just fifty-two, when—I'm thinking it, so I'll just say it—so many mean-spirited people live into their eighties. Do I trust she is in God's loving care, and do I hope this divine care is healing her, just as I hope it will continue to heal me? Definitely.

But my mother was exhausting to live with. She was unpredictably and unapologetically abusive toward me. She expected me somehow to make her happy when she was unwilling or unable to do anything to move herself toward health, even during the times when her energy was relatively high. The fact that these traits are all symptoms of her mental illness helps me, now, to understand them. It doesn't, however, change the fact that my life from the age of twelve has been marked by the trauma of her suicide attempts and, ultimately, her death. And so, do I miss her? Not really. One of my many complicated feelings about my mother—my sorrow, affection, anger, regret—is relief that I don't have to deal with her anymore.

Of course, I do have to deal with my mother. She is the main reason I think so much about suicide. But she is no longer here in the flesh. And although her death left a hole in my life, one of the things that filled that hole was calm where her drama used to be.

Suicide and the Communion of Saints

If you haven't lived with a suicidal person, this may sound harsh, especially coming from someone who is not only a Christian but also a pastor. But it echoes what I have heard from many family members of people who have killed themselves. In my office, with the door closed, as I nodded in understanding while they expressed their relief, they were grateful to have found a safe place to voice it. This relief testifies to a practical reason why care for people at risk from suicide needs to be a communal practice, not solely left up to their closest family and friends—this work is too big for an individual or even a small group of people to handle.

My belief in the communion of saints is what allows me to hope that my mother and I will one day be united in God's all-encompassing love, which will transcend the pains of both our lives and the hurts we inflicted on each other. And my belief in the communion of saints is what convinces me that Christians can hold each other in prayer and care in this life, and can extend that prayer and care to beloved children of God who do not share our faith.

People who have never been suicidal both can and cannot identify with a suicidal person. I think both of these things are true. Putting ourselves in another's shoes is an inherently risky business. As Kathryn Greene-McCreight warns, "Those Christians who have not faced the ravages of mental illness should not be quick with advice to those who do suffer."[3] Even people who have known deep depression, grief, or the disorienting shifts between mania and depression that bipolar disorder brings might not be able to imagine the desire to end their own life. Or, if they can imagine that desire, their vision might falter in the face of actually planning or carrying out the deed.

And yet, those of us who are not suicidal might understand more than we initially realize or willingly acknowledge. We might understand being weary of life or, at least, parts of our lives. We might not be able to imagine where a longed-for, or even desperately needed, change might come from. We might understand the urge to look for a way out. Our preferred way out might be to get drunk or high from time to time, or to binge on shopping, food, or video streaming. These means of escape are, to be sure, less final than suicide. Acknowledging their appeal, however, might offer some glimmer of insight into the desire for escape that animates suicide. To the extent that this insight increases our compassion and lessens our judgmentalism, it can help us be present with people at risk for killing themselves.

People who have pondered suicide do others a favor when they take the risk of sharing their experiences. It can be a blessing to hear what brought them back and what keeps them going, even if just for today, one day at a time.

Clancy Martin, a philosopher who has attempted suicide at least ten times since the age of six, stresses the value of speaking openly about the urge to kill oneself. He suggests "that sometimes we ought to just let our masks down and say, *Hey this is how I'm feeling, and if you're feeling the same way, maybe it will help you to know that you're not alone.*"[4] The hope Martin has for others—that they might find some solidarity in hearing another's story—he also holds for himself: "That the effort to be as truthful as I can about how I am feeling will keep me alive."[5]

Martin has enough experience living with suicidality to know where he can get help when he is able to be truthful and ask for it. There are, however, at least two problems with urging suicidal people to "get help." The first is that their state of mind is, itself, a barrier to reaching out. As we have seen, suicidal people often develop tunnel vision; depression makes it hard to take initiative; psychic pain saps a person's energy. That's why the International Association for Suicide Prevention offers sample text messages a struggling person can copy and send a friend or family member, such as "I don't want to die, but I don't know how to live. Talking with you may help me feel safe. Are you free to talk?" They're trying to lower the barrier to seeking help.

The second problem is that the help available may be deeply inadequate. In 2021, about 17 percent of calls to the national suicide Lifeline were abandoned before the caller connected with a counselor. Text and chat responses were worse, with over 40 percent of texts and almost three-quarters of chats going unanswered. As the *New York Times* reported, "Calls and messages are abandoned for any number of reasons, but in interviews, callers blamed hold times and call center directors bemoaned limited capacity."[6] The implementation of the national 988 crisis line number in 2022, and increased investment in it, reduced the average response time to forty-one seconds. Still, however, "The wait time can vary substantially . . . depending on the location or time of day."[7] And the help received may not actually be helpful. As Victor Armstrong, North Carolina's chief health equity officer, has noted, "Building more of a wrong system is not going to help us [i.e., Black people at risk for suicide]."[8] Crisis line responders need to represent and be equipped to support people of a variety of cultures, and mental health apps need to be constructed with equity and diversity in mind. Further, given that 988 responders can send police to a caller's location if they deem it necessary, the inherently higher risk of sending police to a person of color in crisis has to be acknowledged and better emergency responses found.

And of course, 988 services are free, but in the United States, emergency department visits and mental health care are not. Comedian Maria Bamford, known for drawing on her own mental-health struggles in her work, urges people in distress who lack good options to reach out to anyone who might listen. An atheist who grew up in a Christian family, Bamford's suggestions include, "Tunelessly wail 'Somewhere Over the Rainbow' in the closest church until someone invites you to accept Christ as your personal savior and you get down to the business of getting some ears on your story."[9]

Bamford makes a good point: many people associate church with judgment and shame, but they may also think of it as a place that's supposed to help in an emergency. People in economic need come to churches with past-due water bills, eviction notices, and requests for groceries. What if our worship communities were also places that offered lifelines, fairly literally speaking, for people in danger of killing themselves? If suicide intervention is a matter dear to your heart, you might see if others in your worshiping community feel the same way. Even two or three of you could connect to local organizations working in this area. You might develop a ministry supporting mental health in general, or accompanying people tempted to suicide or survivors of suicide. What that ministry might look like would depend on your local needs and resources.[10]

Not every Christian considers it their personal calling to serve on a mental health support or suicide intervention team. But everyone can gain some basic skills, and everyone can support their church forming a team that's more deeply trained.

A few years ago, I took a two-day suicide intervention first-aid course called Applied Suicide Intervention Skills Training, or ASIST. The most important thing I learned in that course was to ask directly about suicide. Euphemisms like "Are you thinking of hurting yourself?" are not helpful, because a suicidal person might think of suicide, not as harm, but rather as a release from their pain.

When might that question come up? It's important to raise it, Edwin Shneidman writes, "if someone—a patient or colleague or friend or family member—says something that is puzzling or cryptic (in regard to life and death)." The first step would be "to ask what was meant by that remark, and then, if there is any suspicion of suicidal intent, to ask directly, 'Are you talking about suicide?'"[11] Many of us might be afraid of offending someone with that question, or we might be afraid of their answer. If they said yes, what would we do next?

This is a good time to remember that the communion of saints is there for all of us. A suicidal person doesn't have to be alone, and neither do their friends. As we seek to accompany people at risk from suicide, we do so in the company of other Christians. And we are in the company of Jesus, too, who knows the feeling of being abandoned by God and humanity. Seeking support is vital, whether that's a companion to sit and listen to the (possibly) suicidal person together, or someone to listen and care for you after that encounter has ended.

Shneidman has advice, gleaned from his years of research, for supporting someone who is suicidal: "Reduce the pain; remove the blinders; lighten the pressure—all three, even just a little bit."[12] His advice is for therapists, but it holds true for the church. We can listen with kindness, in the hope of alleviating the person's pain even a little bit. We can offer a broader perspective than their tunnel vision allows, praying for them and offering assurances of God's love and the community's support. We can tell them specifically how and why we value their life, even if they don't, in that moment. We can sit with them as they call or text a hotline; call or text for them; or take them to their doctor or the hospital if that is warranted. In so doing, we open their frame of reference beyond themself and beyond the present dreadful moment; we testify to our interconnectedness; and we offer glimpses of God, who sees and loves all of us even when we feel utterly cast out and alone.

Caring for suicidal people might mean doing some things we're not personally comfortable with. For example, one might believe Christians shouldn't own guns. Given that over half of all suicides in the United States are carried out with guns, and that more than half of all gun deaths here are suicides, one might absolutely agree with a plea Clancy Martin has made: "If you are a person who has ever felt the least bit suicidal—or if you are a person who has someone in their life who sometimes you think might suffer depression or might go through a suicidal period—I urge you, I cannot urge you more strongly, get rid of that gun."[13] And yet, if a suicidal friend is not ready to give up their gun, one might encourage them to entrust it temporarily to a church member who is a responsible gun owner.

If people who are depressed or otherwise at risk for suicide are able to be open about how they're feeling, there are many simple ways to show them love. Quaker writer Parker Palmer remembers his friend Bill's way. With Palmer's permission, Bill visited every day to massage his feet for half an hour, speaking few or no words. In the midst of Palmer's deep depression, he says, Bill found the one place in my body where I could still experience feeling—and feel somewhat reconnected with the human race."[14]

Faced with night terrors, religious scholar Monica Coleman "begged" friends to stay overnight on her couch. Those friends, Coleman says, "never asked me anything. They just sat there. That was all I needed: a bodyguard from the dreams."[15]

Suicide and the Communion of Saints

Eventually, though, Coleman stopped calling on her friends to sleep over. She thought she was "a burden" to them, while "they thought the nightmares ended." Eventually, she started to wonder, "What if I just disappeared?" That's why it's important to keep checking on friends with depression or other risk factors for suicide. They may be tempted to disappear, and they may no longer feel able to ask for help.

The help churches provide can be material. Congregants can alleviate the stress experienced by people in a suicidal crisis by bringing meals, running errands, or doing chores; connecting people to therapists who use a sliding scale or might be persuaded to do so; enlisting medical professionals, insurance workers, lawyers, or others in the congregation to navigate the health-care system; or sending restaurant gift certificates or cash.

When I was a child, we weren't part of a church network. My mother was raised in the church but had no adult relationship with it. My father attended weekly Catholic Mass, but his relationship with his parish was so minimal I don't think his priest would have recognized him on the street. True to our family tradition of denial, none of my mother's relatives ever brought over so much as a casserole when she was in crisis. What a difference it would have made for me, not to mention my parents, for our struggle to be acknowledged and material support to be offered in a matter-of-fact way. I came to the church as an adult, after my mother died. I was able to care for myself after her death, in large part, because I was the beneficiary of her life insurance. (It's not usually true that suicide invalidates life insurance; typically, claims are paid as long as the policy was purchased at least two years before the suicide.) Her insurance paid for massage therapy, psychotherapy, and dinners out, and has enabled me to offer material support to others in need, giving them a measure of the breathing room my family lacked.

The help the church provides can be spiritual, too. Our communal practices of prayer and worship can be the habits that uphold us in a crisis, especially when we are trying to support someone else. Christian writer Kathleen Norris experienced this when her husband was hospitalized after a suicide attempt. For years, Norris had made regular retreats with the Benedictine monastic community near her home in South Dakota. With her monk companions, Norris had prayed the psalms over and over. During her husband's suicidal crisis, as she was hit by other, mundane stressors like her computer breaking down, Norris wrote, "If someone had handed me a psalter at that moment, I would likely have thrown it across the room. Yet I went back to the psalms at bedtime that night, and in the morning. I owed so much to them, and to the monastic communities that pray them faithfully, day in, day out."[16]

Norris was held by a community that had taught her to pray the psalms, that was praying them in their house as she prayed in her room alone, that was united through space and time with other people who offered those same prayers in worship and in private devotions. She was held by the communion of saints.

Ken Baldwin's experience of surviving his leap off the Golden Gate Bridge seems to have cured his suicidality, but it remains true that one of the strong risk factors for death by suicide is a previous attempt. There are other risk factors. As the American Foundation for Suicide Prevention says, "No one takes their life for a single reason. Life stresses combined with known risk factors, such as childhood trauma, substance use—or even chronic physical pain—can contribute to someone taking their life."[17]

This reality is what makes me uncomfortable with the term "suicide prevention": none of us can fully prevent another person's actions. In the end, our efforts may come to naught. The person we accompany, the person for whom we care, may kill themself anyway.

When we care for someone who is suicidal, we have to acknowledge the possibility that they may take their own life despite all their efforts, and ours; despite all their prayers, and ours.

I never forget this. When a friend called to ask my advice after learning that his father planned to kill himself, we developed a plan together. (He decided that the safest option for his father, who was in a different country, was to call the police in that location. Others might make a different decision.) Before we ended our call, I took a deep breath and told my friend that I affirmed his choice. Doing what he could to interrupt his father's plan might well save his life. And I also took care to tell him that if this plan were interrupted, his father might still kill himself in the future. If so, that wouldn't be my friend's fault; he would have done what he could, when he could. Thankfully, his father went on to live several more years, and did not die by suicide.

Even when a person does ultimately kill themself, we can give thanks for the years they lived. My mother was thirty-six years old when she made her first suicide attempt I know of, and fifty-two when she died. Whatever the challenges of our relationship, I trust I am better off having lost her as an adult rather than as a child on the brink of adolescence. Those sixteen years brought many good things to my mother, to me, and to other members of her community. Those years matter; how much, only God truly knows.

Part Two. The Communion of Saints

That's why I think it's important for Christians to keep advocating for measures that make suicide less likely. As a person bereaved by suicide, I take this personally. I stood in my kitchen yelling at the radio on the evening in 2014 when National Public Radio reported that the Golden Gate Bridge's board of directors had finally voted to install stainless-steel nets around the bridge. I wasn't yelling because of their vote; I was yelling because the directors had taken so long to act. They had approved the idea in 2008, but without funding the nets. The project, therefore, had remained simply an idea, while forty-six people in 2013 had died after jumping off the bridge (bringing the total to at least sixteen hundred since the Golden Gate opened in 1937).[18] The primary objections to installing safety nets had been that they would mar the bridge's appearance and diminish its historical integrity, and that suicidal people would simply go elsewhere to end their lives.

As evidenced by the epithets I hurled at my radio, I have no patience for the first two objections, measured against the value of human life. The third just isn't true. The Golden Gate Bridge authority has made a point of countering that false impression, stating on their website, "The 1978 Seiden study at the Golden Gate Bridge showed that 90 percent of those stopped from jumping did not later die by suicide or other violent means." Further, "A Harvard School of Public Health article reviewing numerous studies [into the twenty-first century] showed more broadly that 'Nine out of ten people who attempt suicide and survive will not go on to die by suicide at a later date.'"[19] Three things are true: any suicide attempt may be lethal, and a previous suicide attempt is one of the strongest predictors of death by suicide, so it's vital to try to prevent or interrupt attempts. And most people who attempt do not die by suicide, so it's vital to do what we can to increase the likelihood that people will survive attempts.

As the communion of saints seeks to affirm the worth of people at risk for suicide or harmed by it, and to accompany them in their pain, one of the most important things we can do is to avoid the temptation to offer easy answers. Parker Palmer remarks, "I can tell you what I did to survive and, eventually, to thrive—but I cannot tell you why I was able to do those things before it was too late." This not-knowing has made him humble. In conversation with a fellow Christian "who had wrestled with depression for much of her adult life," who asked him, "Why do some people kill themselves yet others get well?," Palmer replied simply, "I have no idea. I really have no idea." Later, he regretted his simple answer, until his acquaintance wrote to say those few words had given her hope: "My response had given her an alternative to the cruel 'Christian explanations' common in the church to which she belonged—that people who take their lives lack faith or good works or some other redeeming virtue that might move God to rescue them. My not knowing had freed her to stop judging herself for being depressed and to stop believing that God was judging her. As a result, her depression had lifted a bit."[20]

Sitting with, praying for, showing up for people affected by suicide: these are marvelously simple and terribly demanding things to do. That's why we need the support of a communion to do them. And we need that communion, too, when our interventions don't go the way we hoped, and we lose someone to suicide.

CHAPTER EIGHT

Remembering God's People Who Die by Suicide

I'm winding my way through the mountains of North Carolina, on the way to meet my family at a cabin in the woods. The CD in the player starts up a jaunty zydeco-infused beat: it's Steve Earle's version of his son Justin Townes Earle's 2010 song "Harlem River Blues." Despite the "blues" in its title, it's quite likely the most cheerful song ever written about suicide: a musical farewell offered as the narrator makes his way to the bridge where he has decided to end his life. Anticipating the release to come, the narrator's mood becomes brighter the closer he gets to the Harlem River. A decade after the song's original release, Steve Earle recorded it for his album *J. T.*, a fund-raiser for the daughter Justin left behind when he died accidentally from using fentanyl-laced cocaine.

Familiar as I am with the son's version of the song, a difference in the father's arrangement catches my ear. Like Justin, Steve has backup singers join him on the chorus, where the narrator cheerily repeats his intention to let the river's "dirty water" absorb him into a final embrace. But while Justin's voice continues strong to the very end of his version, Steve's drops suddenly out of his. His choir of backup singers picks up his refrain about the release to be found in death, repeating it in the face of the lead vocalist's silence, until the music dies away.

I press "repeat" on that song for the final half hour of my drive, fumbling to understand why this version of it moves me so deeply. It's not simply that a father is performing his son's song about self-inflicted death mere months after the son's actual passing—not that there's anything simple about that. What's hitting me is something about the song's arrangement, its vocal harmonies.

Finally, I realize what that something is. Justin Earle's narrator is still alive when the song ends; he's belting out the lyrics up until the very last note. He sounds eager to end his life that night, but as the music fades away, we don't know for sure that he will. At the end of the song, his voice remains strong. He might yet change his mind.

In contrast, when Justin's father sings "Harlem River Blues," the narrator's voice vanishes before the song ends. He has completed the act he announced with such bravado.

But the grace in Steve's arrangement is that the narrator's song doesn't end there. The voices that joined him partway through keep singing after he has taken his leave.[1]

Are those voices a choir of angels, telling him at the end that they accept him as he is? Are they fellow souls who have traveled their own version of his road, joining his song in solidarity?

I don't know. I don't care. What moves me is that, after the shock of realizing the narrator had actually carried out his plan—I closed my eyes for just a moment, before remembering I was at the wheel on a mountain road—I received the consolation of knowing the person who had so eagerly sought out his own death may have met it alone, but he was not forsaken. When he could no longer make a sound, others took up his blues. They told his story. And maybe it was their story too.

Their story, forever intertwined with the stories of the people they left behind.

Part Two. The Communion of Saints

―※―

When someone dies by suicide, after the initial shock has passed, the question of the funeral comes up. How should the person be laid to rest? What should be said about them? How honest should survivors be? When my mother died, a number of her friends told me, "You know, you can just say she had a massive heart attack." My reaction was the opposite: having grown up in a family that refused to acknowledge the toll depression and suicidality had taken on us all, and finally in a position to exercise agency, I was determined to tell the truth. The father of a close friend validated my decision. When my friend called him to share my sad news, he urged her to encourage me to be honest about my mother's death. Although he didn't say so explicitly, his sense of urgency was rooted in the loss of his own father to suicide, and his family's repression of the truth. He had lived silently with the repercussions for decades, never speaking directly about how his father had died. But even as he lived with that unmentionable pain, he wanted something healthier for me.

I was grateful, too, for the ministrations of an acquaintance of my mother, a kind and practical Baptist pastor named Andrew. My mother had a difficult relationship with the church, rarely setting foot in one after graduating from high school and being emancipated from her mother's rules. But she and Andrew had a warm relationship, and when he offered to conduct her funeral, I was grateful for his guidance. I didn't care for everything Andrew said about my mother in his funeral address, like referring to her tendency to "get stuck on her own hurting" as "a tragic character flaw." But I appreciated his openness about the fact that her death was a suicide, from his opening remarks: "Friends, I know that we are hurting a great deal today. If there were words to take away all of your pain, I would surely say them; if there were a reason for this tragedy, I would surely explain; and if there were some prayer I could utter that would bring Cathie back to be with us today, then she would be here. But of course there are none of these."

And I appreciated the encouragement, even absolution, Andrew obliquely aimed at me, acknowledging my need to distance myself from my mother. I had done that literally, moving to the United States for my doctoral program rather than enrolling in the university an hour from her home, which had offered me a more generous fellowship. Andrew noted that, from what he knew of my mother, it seemed that her "ideal daughter" "would be like a loving teddy bear or one of her beloved animals" in whom she could "hide all of her cares and burdens." But, he added, "Children are not born just to make parents happy, but to make a life for themselves." He implicitly gave me his blessing to go on doing that, and I was grateful.

It was after my mother's death that I started attending church, eventually making my way to the Anglican Communion.[2] In the tradition in which I now serve, the burial rite is an Easter liturgy, focused on the resurrection. It offers room for lament while focusing on the hope that we will live again in communion with each other and with the triune God. The commendation at the end of the liturgy is the same for everyone: "Into your hands, O merciful Savior, we commend your servant. Acknowledge, we humbly beseech you, a sheep of your own fold, a lamb of your own flock, a sinner of your own redeeming. Receive [them] into the arms of your mercy, into the blessed rest of everlasting peace, and into the glorious company of the saints in light. Amen."[3] Our rite of burial for a person who did not profess the Christian faith offers substantively the same hope, as in this prayer: "Almighty God, we entrust all who are dear to us to your never-failing

Part Two. The Communion of Saints

care and love, for this life and the life to come, knowing that you are doing for them better things than we can desire or pray for; through Jesus Christ our Lord. Amen."[4]

The focus on resurrection that the Anglican funeral rite shares with other Christian traditions reassures me. It reminds worshipers that we are all sinners beloved by God, and it keeps our focus on God's love and our hope as embodied in Jesus Christ. Our primary attention is not devoted to the deceased. And yet, the rite honors the person we have lost: through the prayers, readings, music, and flowers we choose; sometimes through eulogies or other memorials or thanksgivings; and in the homily, as the preacher relates the life of the departed to the gospel.

Pastoral theologian Loren Townsend offers some practical advice for preaching the funeral of a person who died by suicide. He suggests asking the family, "What would you like me to say about [the deceased]?," "Are there things you want to be sure I say?," and "Are there things you want to be sure I don't say?"[5] These are helpful questions for any funeral preacher, but they're particularly relevant after a suicide. Family members want the deceased to be remembered for more than their manner of death; they may want the funeral to serve as something of a plea to people considering suicide; they may fear saying too much, hurting the deceased's reputation or focusing on death and despair rather than on hope. Townsend recommends listening carefully to the various needs and interests family members may express. When those members "cannot agree on how much to reveal about a suicide," he says "pastors must err on behalf of the most vulnerable in the system."[6] The preacher must thread a thin needle: in the face of denial, it's not their place to insist on "public truth telling" in the name of "healing." Simultaneously, however, "a funeral service must be contextually coherent enough to offer comfort and hope to those who know they are surviving a suicide."[7] Yet another reason why clergy need supportive colleagues, spiritual directors, and therapists: rising to these challenges in caring for others can take a toll if we have no one with whom to process them. Obtaining support for ourselves allows us to remain compassionate and sensitive to others' needs, and to offer support without falling apart or imposing our needs unduly on the people we serve.

My mother's parents did not travel from Scotland to Canada for their daughter's midwinter funeral (although her mother did attend her burial, which had to be delayed until the spring thaw). I don't know what I might have done differently if they had been present. I might have asked Andrew to reduce the number of words he devoted to the reality that my mother's death had been a suicide. But I believe I still would have asked him to address that fact directly, so determined was I to break the silence around mental illness that had traumatized my family—and me—so deeply. My grandparents' pain was a terrible thing to witness, but they were going to feel that pain regardless. And others besides me might be helped by telling the truth.

After attorney, television journalist, and former Miss USA Cheslie Kryst killed herself in 2022, her family and church fellowship achieved a delicate balance of praising and beseeching God, celebrating Kryst's life, and advocating for suicidal people and others at risk, in her public memorial service. A video of Kryst showed her speaking about the importance of being a role model for young Black women and women of color. "We *can* support each other," Kryst stated emphatically. "We can *all* be successful." Thanking everyone who had prayed for her family, and asking that prayers continue, Kryst's mother, April Simpkins, said of her daughter, "She is forever my baby girl, and I'm gonna miss all of her, and her living example of a pure giving heart." Neither Simpkins nor any other speaker tried to resolve the contradictions of Kryst's life and death. They praised her virtues, they acknowledged that she had suffered from depression, and they used the occasion to encourage support for people who might be considering suicide.

At the close of her remarks, Simpkins offered "three calls to action": "First, take care of your mental health." To anyone who had already chosen to seek counseling, she said, "I'm proud of you." Second, she asked participants to add the national suicide prevention hotline number to their phones. And third, she suggested, "Honor Cheslie by becoming an ally for a community that needs support. A community you neither belong to, nor benefit from. Be selfless, like Cheslie." The service's closing prayer asked God, "the great comforter, [who comes] to us in times of trouble and in times of need," for help "to carry your joy" and to seek and offer support as needed.[8]

Cheslie Kryst's family chose to actively and deliberately undermine the pernicious myth that Black women don't experience mental illness, are too "strong" to need help, and aren't at risk for suicide.[9] Although the suicide rate for African American women is lower than for other groups, it increased sharply between 1999 and 2020, especially among those in their teens and twenties.[10] It seems undeniable that structural racism, and the new arenas that opened up for racism as the Internet expanded over those two decades, play key roles in this increase. Accordingly, any social or personal strategy to reduce suicide's toll will have to be multifaceted. Black theologian Monica Coleman found that was the case in her own journey with mental illness and suicidal ideation, recovering from sexual assault and learning about the legacy of suicide in her own family. "With therapists, medication, meaningful studies, a small church community, a pastor who cared, friends who understood, and a name for my condition," she has written, "God was knitting me back together."[11]

Knowing what to tell children can be most challenging. When the time came to tell my daughter—years after my mother's death—how that absent grandmother had died, I used language taught me by a friend whose partner died by suicide when their daughter was a kindergartner. I said she had "made herself die." I also said I didn't know why, exactly, my mother had done that, but that she did suffer from a sickness called depression, which sometimes leads people to end their own lives. I took care to say that depression is not like regular sadness, that it's OK to be sad, and that my mother's death made me sad. I told her suicide is a terrible thing to do, and that we don't stop loving people who die that way. And I speak about my mother from time to time, especially noting the gifts she passed on to me, like her sense of humor and her delight in everyday pleasures. All these feelings, together, can sound complicated. It's important for children to know that feelings can be complicated, and that we can express them both to other people and to God. It's up to adults to create spaces where children can bravely express their feelings, to other people and to God, and feel heard and held as they do so.

Sometimes parents fear that talking about suicide will put the idea into their child's head. That's not true. Children and teenagers hear about suicide on the news and at school. Because of the importance of peer relationships to teenagers, suicide contagion among adolescents is a documented reality, although it is neither inevitable nor widespread. If a respected peer role model dies by suicide, an adolescent who is also experiencing anxiety, depression, or other painful distress might be more likely to see suicide as one way to end their own suffering.[12] That's why it's important for parents to talk directly about suicide with their children, and for communities to offer mental health resources and other forms of support that parents can't (or sometimes won't) provide on their own. The church can help with all of this.

―――

What might have been helpful to me, in the years following my mother's death, was a service like the one that has been offered at St. Martin-in-the-Fields in London. Called "Time to Talk" and offered "to stand in solidarity with those affected by suicide," the service is aimed at three groups. First, the parents of people who had taken their own life; then, other family members; and finally, "those who had themselves attempted suicide, often more than once, and had reached a place where their life was no longer in the same degree of crisis and were willing to speak about what they had been through and offer support to those whose stories had worked out differently."[13] The service's organizers realized participants might be suspicious of the church, with good reason. St. Martin's was chosen because of what its vicar, Sam Wells, called its "congregation's reputation for humane and sensitive understandings of a whole range of pastoral issues."[14] That is a reputation any church could develop, if it were determined to.

The service leads participants on a three-part journey. First, it "takes seriously and attempts to meet head on the genuine dismay and horror of losing a loved one to suicide. It speaks the language of lament, testimony and pain." Second, it "addresses the more ambivalent experience of attempting suicide and surviving to tell the tale," articulating what might go through their mind in a moment of crisis, and showing "how those thoughts can be modified and even healed."

Third, it "tentatively"—I so appreciate the humility inherent in that word—"hints at solace, in wisdom if not in joy, in solidarity if not in closure, in goodness if not in transformation." Any address or sermon by clergy needs to focus on "tone of voice more than content" and express "compassion and understanding" rather than explicating a biblical text or insisting on a Christian interpretation of suicide. Finally, Wells notes, it's "vital" to provide an opportunity "to gather informally afterwards over coffee."[15]

I have never been offered such a service. In the two decades I have been ordained, my offers to lead one have never been accepted. I can only imagine how helpful a liturgy like this would have been to my mother—except that attending one would have been as unthinkable to her as dropping by a rave. This kind of service would have helped me, however. Fortunately, the church I started attending several months after my mother's death had no qualms about me crying my way through their services for the first year, and it offered both clergy and laypeople who listened kindly and without judgment.

Wells's comment about solace in wisdom, solidarity, and goodness resonates with me when I think of my one group experience of reckoning with suicide: the annual Out of the Darkness Overnight Walk, a fund-raiser for the American Foundation for Suicide Prevention. An entirely secular event, it's characterized by a generosity and an ethic of mutual care that churches would do well to emulate. One Overnight Walk veteran brought a stack of bandannas to give the newcomers who hadn't thought to carry anything with which to wipe their faces over the course of the seventeen-mile trek through Manhattan and Brooklyn. All of us, strangers until that evening, asked each other, "How are you? How is your family?" and stuck around to hear the answer. For long stretches, we trudged along in silent solidarity. The last few

Part Two. The Communion of Saints

miles, I walked with a brother and sister whose father had died when he was a freshman in high school and she was a freshman in college. At the finish line, they introduced me to their mother, who hugged me along with her children. When she exclaimed, "I'm so proud of you guys!" she meant all three of us.

The Overnight Walk's secular nature is a blessing, I think, because it allows more people to be involved and to offer each other support. But as a Christian it makes me sad, too, that the most life-affirming witness I have ever encountered to loving persistence in the face of suicide, filled with mutual vulnerability and support, dedicated to luring as many precious lives back from the brink as possible, had nothing explicitly to do with the church.

Recently, I was terrified that someone dear to me, whose life I value far above my own, would attempt suicide. I did everything I could to ensure they had proper care, and I prayed mightily for them. And then I realized there was one thing left for me to do: I could ask my mother and my biological father to pray for this beloved person.

Asking my mother for help had been a risky venture since I entered my teens. Rarely did she grant my requests; more often, they triggered a litany of my shortcomings. And the man with whom she had conceived me, months before their short marriage dissolved, had given me nothing but his genes: no child support, no contact, ever. I had asked him for one thing, when I was in my forties and he in his seventies: to talk with me about his life with my mother. He turned down that request—which I know he received—by not replying to it. The next I heard of him, he had died of an overdose of the Dilaudid his wife had left behind when cancer took her life a couple of years earlier.

A decade later, in my state of terror, it occurred to me to call upon the two of them to intercede for the person I loved. Maybe they could collaborate on this for me—their last joint project. My request was succinct and not at all elegant: "You two know what it's like to want a way out. And you know suicide is not the way for this person. Please, help them stay here. Help them hold onto life."

Both my mother and my biological father were baptized Christians, but neither of them had practiced the faith for decades before their deaths. The branches of the church in which they were raised would have looked askance at my asking them to intercede. But my own faith gave me hope that they were now experiencing what I hope lies ahead for me: a life of ever-closer communion with God and neighbor, slowly being perfected in love, and joining their prayers to those offered by the living. I trust these two ancestors—with flaws and gifts I share—are still members of the communion of saints, and I hope—sometimes with little conviction, but I still hope—our broken relationships will be healed in God's time. Perhaps this hope, in God rather than in any human, is the best way I can remember both of them.

I can't guarantee that no one I love, or you love, will ever again die by suicide. But I can do what I can to witness to God's love and to the reality that this love connects us all. And I can encourage my fellow Christians to do the same.

Questions to Consider

CHAPTER ONE

1. In reading this chapter, were you reminded of other areas of life where choosing one word over another is important to you, for theological, moral, or other important reasons?
2. In the past, how have you talked about suicide or referred to people who died in this way?
3. How do you imagine talking about suicide in the future? Might the words you choose depend on the situation or to whom you are speaking, or do you believe there are one or two correct words or phrases to use?
4. Can there be any value in attaching shame and the threat of punishment to suicide?

CHAPTER TWO

1. What can the cases of suicide in the Old Testament offer Christians in our ethics and practices around suicide?
2. Reading anew the stories of Judas, what thoughts and feel-

Questions to Consider

ings come up for you? What might you say to him or ask him now, given the opportunity?
3. Did this chapter give you a new perspective on any of the passages it discussed, as you considered them with regard to suicide?
4. Which scriptural stories, passages, or images, mentioned in this chapter or not, have you found helpful in bleak moments?

Chapter Three

1. Did anything you read about Augustine's or Thomas Aquinas's views surprise you?
2. In particular, did it surprise you to read Augustine's assurance that survivors of sexual assault do not bear responsibility for the harm done to them?
3. What, if anything, were you taught about the ethics of suicide as a young person, or as a person new to Christianity?
4. How do you imagine God responds to suicide?

Chapter Four

1. What are your thoughts and feelings as you contemplate "suicide by proxy" and "suicide by lottery"?
2. It is generally no longer true that churches deny full burial rites to people who die by suicide. Do you encounter people who don't realize that is the case? Does your family's oral tradition include memories of relatives, friends, or neighbors who were denied full rites?

Questions to Consider

CHAPTER FIVE

1. What thoughts and feelings come up for you as you consider suicides undertaken in response to cruelty inflicted by others?
2. As a Christian, what do you lament about past practices or beliefs of the church that devalued some human lives and contributed to suicide?
3. Does the church generally, or your branch in particular, hold current practices and beliefs that information in this chapter has you wondering about? How might you think about, pray about, and otherwise act upon those questions?

CHAPTER SIX

1. What do you make of the contrast between what Scripture says are the fruits of the Spirit and the suicidal state of mind?
2. If you have been suicidal in the past, what forms of support were, or would have been, helpful to you? Have you been willing and able to share that insight with others who don't share your experience?
3. If you have never been suicidal, can you identify at all with the desire to disappear, even temporarily?
4. What might you consider saying to, or doing with, someone who feels abandoned by God?
5. How might you pray for someone who is in danger of suicide?

Questions to Consider

Chapter Seven

1. What do you make of the many and sometimes conflicting emotions often experienced by survivors of suicide? If you are not a survivor, can you think of other situations in which you have experienced similarly complicated feelings?
2. What spiritual, material, and other resources might you be able to offer someone in suicidal distress?
3. What forms of support would you need from others in order to support a suicidal person? Where might you turn for them?

Chapter Eight

1. How might you pray for someone who died by suicide? If your beliefs don't affirm praying for the dead, what hope might you hold for a person who died by suicide, and how might you express that hope?
2. If you have lost someone to suicide, how do you remember them? Do you honor their memory in some particular ways?
3. What resources exist in your community for survivors (whether of their own attempts or of another's suicide) to come together to lament, find support, and take constructive action? Are there ways you, your family and friends, or your church community could get involved in existing efforts, or provide for an unmet need?

Acknowledgments

I am grateful to say that the writing of this book was partially funded by a Pastoral Study Project grant from the Louisville Institute. I also give thanks for the Hutson Fund for Clergy Professional Development, established in memory of Kay Swaim Hutson by her husband, Richard, at St. Luke's Episcopal Church in Durham, North Carolina.

Parts of my discussion of the American Foundation for Suicide Prevention's Out of the Darkness Overnight Walk in chapter 8 originally appeared in Rhonda Mawhood Lee, "Tips for Congregations from an Overnight Walk in Manhattan," *Faith & Leadership* (www.faithandleadership.com), September 6, 2016. Thanks to *Faith & Leadership* for their permission to use this material.

Many thanks to Lisa Ann Cockrel, Jeff Dundas, Claire Galloway, Jenny Hoffman, Amy Kent, Tom Raabe, and their colleagues at Eerdmans, all of whom were generous and supportive throughout the publishing process.

Among the skilled therapists who have helped me over the course of decades, I give thanks for Elaine Crovitz, Edna Goldstaub, Sara Rosenquist, and Irv Rosenstein.

Because she loves Jesus, writing, and me, Lauren F. Winner

Acknowledgments

read the entire manuscript, asked insightful questions, and offered prayer and encouragement over the years I devoted to this book. What a blessing.

In a book full of good sentences, Tiffany Eberle Kriner wrote the best sentence about professing faith that I have ever read. And she has prayed faithfully for and with me; praise be to God.

It's easy for me to be such a firm believer in the communion of saints, and in the friendships that can flourish inside and outside the church, because I have been so blessed by them. For their support over the years (or decades), I give thanks for and to Javier Almendárez-Bautista, Sarah and Rich Ball-Damberg, Tammy Bouchelle and Holly Martin, David Carter and Alice Novak, Ann Claycombe and Jacob Selwood, Michael B. Curry, Lisa and Tommy D'Amico, Éric Darier, Cathy Deats, Kirsten Delegard and James Eli Shiffer, Kathleen DuVal and Marty Smith, Deborah Finkel, Marjorie George, Christine Gilsenan, Patrice Gopo, Michael Green, Cheri Harper, Donna Hicks, Julia Hoyle and Patty Michaels, Michael Buerkel Hunn, Nathan Kirkpatrick, Michelle Lanier, Adriane Lentz-Smith and Christian Lentz, Janna Louie, Catherine Massey, Kathryn Mathers and Jehangir Malegam, Malissa McLeod and Brett Whelan, the Morgan-Tyson family, Kirk Royal, Kelly Ryan, Gwen Schulman, Mark Sheftall, Kara Slade, the Slattery-Salemson family, Caleb Tabor, Anthony Vinson, OSB, Joanna Walsh, fcJ, Katie Westermann, Kate Wisz, and Stephanie Yancy.

An inspiring scholar, teacher, and lover of life, Wayne E. Lee has been my friend longer than almost anyone. For him and for our family, I am most grateful.

Thanks be to God.

Notes

Forewarning

1. Centers for Disease Control and Prevention data show there were 48,183 suicides in the United States in 2021. "Suicide Data and Statistics" (2021), Centers for Disease Control and Prevention, https://tinyurl.com/yzjzn556.
2. "Suicide," World Health Organization, August 28, 2023, https://tinyurl.com/3e9wdm8r.

Introduction

1. Martin Luther, "Table Talk," entry 222 (April 7, 1532), in *Luther's Works, American Edition*, vol. 54, ed. and trans. Theodore G. Tappert (Philadelphia: Fortress, 1967), 29, also accessed at Ethics of Suicide Digital Archive, May 21, 2015, https://tinyurl.com/yk3vvmu4.
2. I was raised by my mother and her second husband, to whom I refer as my father, who died of cancer five years before my mother's passing.
3. The link between depression and suicidality is attested in many sources, as is the role other factors can play. See "Risk Factors, Protective Factors, and Warning Signs," American Founda-

tion for Suicide Prevention, accessed July 17, 2024, https://tinyurl.com/2wdhxcxm.

4. 1 Cor. 15:14. All quotations from the Bible come from the New Revised Standard Version, unless otherwise indicated.

5. 1 Cor. 15:20–22.

6. Rom. 7:15.

7. Quoted as an epigraph to Clancy Martin, *How Not to Kill Yourself: A Portrait of the Suicidal Mind* (New York: Pantheon, 2023).

8. Quoted in Eddie S. Glaude Jr., *Begin Again: James Baldwin's America and Its Urgent Lessons for Our Own* (New York: Crown, 2020), 34.

9. James Baldwin, *Another Country*, in James Baldwin, *Early Novels and Stories* (New York: Library of America, 1998), 472–73.

Chapter One

1. English shares the expression "to commit suicide" with other Germanic languages, like German and Dutch. In other languages, like French, Spanish, and Italian, one can simply use "suicide" as a verb, to say someone "suicided." Some suicide-prevention organizations now encourage English speakers to adopt that expression.

2. Anton J. L. van Hooff, "A Longer Life for 'Suicide': When Was the Latin Word for Self-Murderer Invented?" *Romanische Forschungen* 102, no. 2/3 (1990): 255–59.

3. Augustine, *Concerning the City of God against the Pagans*, trans. Henry Bettenson (New York: Penguin Classics, 1984), 1.17, p. 27. The original Latin reads "qui se ipsum occidit, homicida est."

4. Hooff, "A Longer Life for 'Suicide,'" 257.

5. Clancy Martin's repeated references to his "failed" suicide attempts in his searingly honest memoir are, in my view, irresponsible blemishes on an otherwise helpful book, *How Not to Kill Yourself*.

6. "Safe Reporting Guidelines for Media," American Founda-

tion for Suicide Prevention, accessed July 17, 2024, https://tinyurl.com/2p4yrf9c.

Chapter Two

1. Gen. 9:6.
2. Exod. 20:13.
3. Judg. 9:53–54.
4. 1 Kings 16:18–19.
5. 2 Sam. 17:23.
6. Robert Alter, *The Hebrew Bible*, vol. 2, *Prophets: A Translation with Commentary* (New York: Norton, 2019), 382n23.
7. Judg. 16:28, 30.
8. Judg. 16:18–30.
9. Heb. 11:32–34.
10. Augustine, *City of God* 1.21, p. 32.
11. Robert Alter, *The Hebrew Bible*, vol. 3, *The Writings: A Translation with Commentary* (New York: Norton, 2019), 459.
12. Job 3, passim.
13. Phil. 1:21–24.
14. Most notably, Arthur J. Droge, "Mori Lucrum: Paul and Ancient Theories of Suicide," *Novum Testamentum* 30, no. 3 (July 1988): 263–86.
15. N. Clayton Croy, "'To Die Is Gain' (Philippians 1:19–26): Does Paul Contemplate Suicide?" *Journal of Biblical Literature* 122, no. 3 (Autumn 2003): 525.
16. Croy, "'To Die Is Gain,'" 530.
17. Augustine, *City of God* 1.17, p. 27.
18. Catherine of Siena, *The Dialogue: A Conversation with God on Living Your Spiritual Life to the Fullest* (Gastonia, NC: TAN Books, 2010), 53.

19. Matt. 27:3–5.

20. Acts 1:18.

21. Dante, *Inferno*, canto 34.

22. Alexander Murray, *Suicide in the Middle Ages*, vol. 2, *The Curse on Self-Murder* (Oxford: Oxford University Press, 2000), 332.

23. Murray, *Suicide in the Middle Ages*, 2:330.

24. Willie James Jennings, *Acts* (Louisville: Westminster John Knox, 2017), 25.

25. Hagar's story appears in Gen. 16 and Gen. 21:9–21.

26. Gen. 16:10.

27. Jessica Coblentz, *Dust in the Blood: A Theology of Life with Depression* (Collegeville, MN: Liturgical Press, 2022), 162–63. A foundational study of the story of Hagar, which influenced Coblentz, is Delores S. Williams, *Sisters in the Wilderness: The Challenge of Womanist God-Talk* (Maryknoll, NY: Orbis Books, 1993).

28. Coblentz, *Dust in the Blood*, 165.

29. Coblentz, *Dust in the Blood*, 166.

30. David Finnegan-Hosey, *Christ on the Psych Ward* (New York: Church Publishing, 2018), 84–85.

31. Lauren F. Winner, *Wearing God: Clothing, Laughter, Fire, and Other Overlooked Ways of Meeting God* (New York: HarperOne, 2015).

32. Jesus prays this prayer in Mark 14:36 and 14:39, Matt. 26:39, and Luke 22:42. In John 12:27, he dismisses the idea of asking God to save him from death. It is still clear, however, that he is not seeking death, but rather sees it as a vital part of God's plan for salvation.

Chapter Three

1. Augustine, *City of God* 1.20, p. 31.

2. Ambrose of Milan, "On Virgins: Letter to Marcellina," Ethics of Suicide Digital Archive, May 21, 2015, https://tinyurl.com/5yexdzj5.

Notes to Pages 33–42

3. Cited in Murray, *Suicide in the Middle Ages*, 2:100–101.

4. For Augustine, this authority can be transferred to human beings under limited circumstances, for example, to soldiers fighting a just war.

5. Augustine, *City of God* 1.19, p. 30.

6. Alexander Murray, "Suicide in the Middle Ages," *Synergy* 18, no. 5 (Fall/Winter 2012): 4.

7. Augustine, *City of God* 1.27, p. 38.

8. Tweet by @Acilius, January 31, 2022. Used with the author's permission.

9. Augustine, "On Free Choice of the Will," Ethics of Suicide Digital Archive, May 21, 2015, https://tinyurl.com/3rwkthdb.

10. Augustine, "On Free Choice of the Will."

11. All quotes from Thomas Aquinas in this chapter come from his *Summa Theologiae*, New Advent, accessed July 17, 2024, https://tinyurl.com/5n6j5f6r.

12. Richard A. Heckler, *Waking Up Alive: The Descent, the Suicide Attempt & the Return to Life* (New York: G. P. Putnam's Sons, 1994), 119–20.

13. John Donne, "Devotions upon Emergent Occasions," Meditation XVII, in *The Complete Poetry and Selected Prose of John Donne*, ed. Charles M. Coffin (New York: Random House Modern Library, 2001), 446.

14. Augustine, *City of God* 1.17, p. 27.

Chapter Four

1. Dante, *Inferno*, canto 13.

2. Murray, *Suicide in the Middle Ages*, 2:267, 272.

3. *Catechism of the Catholic Church* (Vatican City: Libreria Editrice Vaticana, 1993), paragraphs 2282–2283.

Notes to Pages 43–49

4. Murray, *Suicide in the Middle Ages*, 2:267, 272.

5. William Shakespeare, *Hamlet*, act 5, scene 1.

6. Luther, "Table Talk," 29.

7. Kay Redfield Jamison, *Night Falls Fast: Understanding Suicide* (New York: Knopf, 1999), 16.

8. Heiko A. Oberman, *Luther: Man between God and the Devil*, trans. Eileen Walliser-Schwarzbart (New Haven: Yale University Press, 1989), 320–21.

9. Oberman, *Luther*, 323–24.

10. Oberman, *Luther*, 324.

11. Luther, "Table Talk."

12. Alexander Murray, *Suicide in the Middle Ages*, vol. 1, *The Violent against Themselves* (Oxford: Oxford University Press, 1998), 369–71.

13. Kathy Stuart, *Suicide by Proxy in Early Modern Germany: Crime, Sin, and Salvation* (Cham, Switzerland: Palgrave Macmillan, 2023), 81–82.

14. Kathy Stuart, "Suicides by Proxy: The Unintended Consequences of Public Executions in Eighteenth-Century Germany," *Central European History* 41, no. 3 (September 2008): 413–14, 421.

15. Stuart, *Suicide by Proxy*, 19–24.

16. Robert Hughes, *The Fatal Shore: The Epic of Australia's Founding* (New York: Vintage Books, 1988), 467.

17. Hughes, *The Fatal Shore*, 468.

Chapter Five

1. Marcus Rediker, *The Slave Ship: A Human History* (New York: Penguin Books, 2008), 17–19. The man and his entire family were sold onto the slave ship in late 1783 or early 1784.

Notes to Pages 50–53

2. Terri L. Snyder, *The Power to Die: Slavery and Suicide in British North America* (Chicago: University of Chicago Press, 2015), 23.

3. Rediker, *The Slave Ship*, 289–90.

4. Yolanda Pierce, *In My Grandmother's House: Black Women, Faith, and the Stories We Inherit* (Minneapolis: Broadleaf Books, 2021), 159.

5. Willie James Jennings, *The Christian Imagination: Theology and the Origins of Race* (New Haven: Yale University Press, 2010), 179.

6. William D. Piersen, *From Africa to America: African American History from the Colonial Era to the Early Republic, 1526–1790* (New York: Twain Publishers, 1996), 32.

7. Jennings, *The Christian Imagination*, 179.

8. Jennings, *The Christian Imagination*, 178.

9. Jennings, *The Christian Imagination*, 178.

10. Snyder, *The Power to Die*, 149.

11. Charles Ball, *Slavery in the United States: A Narrative of the Life and Adventures of Charles Ball* (New York: John S. Taylor, 1837), 69.

12. Cited in Snyder, *The Power to Die*, 149.

13. Harriet Jacobs, *Incidents in the Life of a Slave Girl* (1861; reprint, Mineola, NY: Dover Thrift Editions, 2001), 67.

14. Quoted in Georgia Writers' Project, *Drums and Shadows*, 1940; online at https://tinyurl.com/yxsttbpj. The quote from Wallace Quarterman here has been rendered into standard English.

15. Snyder, *The Power to Die*, 162.

16. Quoted in Snyder, *The Power to Die*, 163.

17. Toni Morrison's comments about flying Africans are on YouTube, at https://tinyurl.com/2ath6n58, accessed July 18, 2024. Rhiannon Giddens's song "We Could Fly," from her 2017 album *Freedom Highway*, is one among many beautiful artistic affirmations of Black people's ability to fly.

18. Toni Morrison, *Song of Solomon* (New York: Knopf, 1977), 326–27.

19. "Suicide Data and Statistics" (2021), Centers for Disease Control and Prevention, https://tinyurl.com/37pnha5v.

20. Tanya Talaga, *All Our Relations: Indigenous Trauma in the Shadow of Colonialism* (London: Scribe, 2020), 13.

21. Helen Milroy, quoted in Talaga, *All Our Relations*, 15.

22. "Suicide Statistics," American Foundation for Suicide Prevention, May 19, 2023 (data are from 2021), https://tinyurl.com/2mwruab7; "Suicide Data and Statistics" (2021).

23. "National Survey on LGBTQ Mental Health 2021," Trevor Project, https://tinyurl.com/3mcfxe4h.

24. Arielle H. Sheftall, "The Tragedy of Black Youth Suicide," *American Association of Medical Colleges News*, April 11, 2023, https://tinyurl.com/4ytujr3t.

25. "Suicide Data and Statistics," Centers for Disease Control and Prevention, reviewed November 29, 2023, https://tinyurl.com/yzjzn556.

26. Quoted in David Paulsen, "Visit to Castle's Dungeon in Ghana Offers ACC Lessons on Church's Complicity in the Transatlantic Slave Trade," Episcopal News Service, February 15, 2023, https://tinyurl.com/mr29sf4k.

27. "Suicide Statistics," American Foundation for Suicide Prevention.

28. Johann Hari, *Lost Connections: Why You're Depressed and How to Find Hope* (New York: Bloomsbury, 2019), 182.

29. Hari, *Lost Connections*, 188.

30. "Mental Health," World Health Organization, June 17, 2022, https://tinyurl.com/2a52n6ak.

31. Albert Camus, *The Myth of Sisyphus and Other Essays* (New York: Vintage Books, 1991; original 1942), 3.

Chapter Six

1. The Episcopal Church, *The Book of Common Prayer and Administration of the Sacraments and Other Rites and Ceremonies of the Church: Together with the Psalter or Psalms of David according to the Use of the Episcopal Church* (New York: Church Publishing, 1979), 713. Online at https://bcponline.org/.

2. Scholar Robert Alter notes that in the original Hebrew, the final line sounds even more fragmented, as if the singer is no longer capable of forming a coherent utterance: "My friends—utter darkness" (just two words in Hebrew). "The sense," Alter observes, "is either that the speaker's friends, because they have rejected him and withdrawn their presence from him, are nothing but darkness to him, or that now the only 'friend' he has is darkness." Robert Alter, *The Book of Psalms: A Translation with Commentary* (New York: Norton, 2007), 310.

3. I write about praying the psalms and the value of the range of emotions expressed there in *Seek and You Will Find: Discovering a Practice of Prayer* (Cincinnati: Forward Movement, 2021).

4. Kathryn Greene-McCreight, *Darkness Is My Only Companion: A Christian Response to Mental Illness* (Grand Rapids: Brazos, 2006), 13.

5. Greene-McCreight, *Darkness Is My Only Companion*, 14.

6. Greene-McCreight, *Darkness Is My Only Companion*, 25.

7. Gal. 5:22–23.

8. Greene-McCreight, *Darkness Is My Only Companion*, 29–30.

9. Parker J. Palmer, "My Spiritual Journey," *Patheos*, November 18, 2020, https://tinyurl.com/2ka5mrfa.

10. Parker J. Palmer, *Let Your Life Speak: Listening for the Voice of Vocation* (San Francisco: Jossey-Bass, 2000), 58.

11. Gillian Marchenko, *Still Life: A Memoir of Living Fully with Depression* (Downers Grove, IL: InterVarsity Press, 2016), 11.

12. "Pastors Have Congregational and, for Some, Personal Experience with Mental Illness," Lifeway Research, August 2, 2022, https://tinyurl.com/bdzfeuhv. The phone survey of one thousand Protestant pastors was conducted in September 2021.

13. "Pastors Have Congregational and, for Some, Personal Experience with Mental Illness."

14. Coblentz, *Dust in the Blood*, 58.

15. Quoted in Coblentz, *Dust in the Blood*, 58.

16. Coblentz, *Dust in the Blood*, 58–59.

17. Coblentz, *Dust in the Blood*, 64.

18. Greene-McCreight, *Darkness Is My Only Companion*, 115–16.

19. Jim Forest, *All Is Grace: A Biography of Dorothy Day* (Maryknoll, NY: Orbis Books, 2011), 292. Apparently, Dorothy was given to reminding people that God is not bound by time.

20. Dorothy Day, "On Pilgrimage," *Catholic Worker*, April 1948, 1, 2, 11; online at https://tinyurl.com/ytxzrcju.

21. Forest, *All Is Grace*, 54.

22. *Catechism of the Catholic Church*, paragraphs 2282–2283.

23. John Bateson, *The Final Leap: Suicide on the Golden Gate Bridge* (Oakland: University of California Press, 2012), 111. Ken Baldwin made his attempt in 1985 at the age of twenty-eight.

24. Edwin S. Shneidman, *The Suicidal Mind* (New York: Oxford University Press, 1996), 133–34.

25. Shneidman, *The Suicidal Mind*, 59.

26. Coblentz, *Dust in the Blood*, 46.

27. Lisa Stevenson, *Life beside Itself: Imagining Care in the Canadian Arctic* (Oakland: University of California Press, 2014), 10.

28. Stevenson, *Life beside Itself*, 10.

29. Stevenson, *Life beside Itself*, 173.

30. Stevenson, *Life beside Itself*, 96.

31. Rom. 8:22.

32. Tiffany Eberle Kriner, *In Thought, Word, and Seed: Reckonings from a Midwest Farm* (Grand Rapids: Eerdmans, 2023), 86.

Chapter Seven

1. The Episcopal Church, *The Book of Common Prayer and Administration of the Sacraments*, 862.
2. Elizabeth L. Antus, "'The Silence of the Dead': Remembering Suicide Victims and Reimagining the Communion of Saints," *Theological Studies* 81, no. 2 (2020): 397. I share Antus's practice of praying for the dead. Even Christians who do not share this practice can explicitly include Christians who die by suicide within the communion of saints and affirm that they are in God's hands, as we all are.
3. Greene-McCreight, *Darkness Is My Only Companion*, 21.
4. Martin, *How Not To Kill Yourself*, 153.
5. Martin, *How Not To Kill Yourself*, 222.
6. Steve Eder, "As a Crisis Hotline Grows, So Do Fears It Won't Be Ready," *New York Times*, March 13, 2022, https://tinyurl.com/fk3ap77c.
7. Eder, "As a Crisis Hotline Grows, So Do Fears It Won't Be Ready."
8. Victor Armstrong, MSW, "Coming Together to Prevent Suicide in Black Communities," town hall presented by American Foundation for Suicide Prevention, Facebook Live, February 24, 2022. Armstrong is deputy secretary for health equity and chief health equity officer, North Carolina Department of Health and Human Services.
9. Maria Bamford, *Sure, I'll Join Your Cult: A Memoir of Mental Illness and the Quest to Belong Anywhere* (New York: Gallery Books, 2023), 255.
10. Helpful resources include Rachel A. Keefe, *The Lifesaving Church: Faith Communities and Suicide Prevention* (Des Peres, MO: Chalice, 2018), and Karen Mason, *The Essentials of Suicide Prevention: A Blueprint for Churches* (Eugene, OR: Cascade, 2023).

11. Shneidman, *The Suicidal Mind*, 52.

12. Shneidman, *The Suicidal Mind*, 139.

13. Terry Gross, "A Survivor of Multiple Suicide Attempts Explains 'How Not to Kill Yourself,'" National Public Radio, April 5, 2023, https://tinyurl.com/mr3jpnx4. The statistics about guns and suicide come from Emily Baumgaertner, "U.S. Rate of Suicide by Firearm Reaches Record Level," *New York Times*, November 30, 2023, https://tinyurl.com/bdcsmmjv.

14. Palmer, *Let Your Life Speak*, 63.

15. Monica A. Coleman, *Bipolar Faith: A Black Woman's Journey with Depression and Faith* (Minneapolis: Fortress, 2016), 88.

16. Kathleen Norris, *Acedia & Me: A Marriage, Monks, and a Writer's Life* (reprint, New York: Riverhead Books, 2010), 77–78.

17. "What We've Learned through Research," American Foundation for Suicide Prevention, accessed July 17, 2024, https://tinyurl.com/2fs4xrmt. The Centers for Disease Control and Prevention affirm these findings and elaborate further in "Risk and Protective Factors for Suicide," accessed July 17, 2024, https://tinyurl.com/5n765y6e.

18. Michael Cabanatuan, "Golden Gate Bridge Board OKs $76 Million for Suicide Barrier," *SFGate*, June 28, 2014, https://tinyurl.com/mrxhca9d.

19. "How the Net Works," Golden Gate Bridge Highway & Transportation District, accessed July 24, 2024, https://tinyurl.com/2apvhxuc. The study cited is R. H. Seiden, "Where Are They Now? A Follow-Up Study of Suicide Attempters from the Golden Gate Bridge," *Suicide and Life-Threatening Behavior* 8, no. 4 (Winter 1978): 203–16, https://tinyurl.com/35xs6ntp. The Harvard article cited is "Attempters' Longterm Survival," Harvard T. H. Chan School of Public Health, accessed July 19, 2024, https://tinyurl.com/3rnuyvmw.

20. Palmer, *Let Your Life Speak*, 58–59.

Chapter Eight

1. The two versions are available on a variety of streaming services.

2. I wrote about my journey toward claiming my infant baptism in the wake of my mother's death in "Indissoluble," in *Common Prayer: Reflections on Episcopal Worship*, ed. Joseph S. Pagano and Amy E. Richter (Eugene, OR: Cascade, 2019), 4–11.

3. The Episcopal Church, *The Book of Common Prayer and Administration of the Sacraments*, 499.

4. The Episcopal Church, *The Book of Occasional Services 2022* (New York: Church Publishing, 2022), 235.

5. Loren L. Townsend and Daniel G. Bagby, eds., *Suicide: Pastoral Responses* (Nashville: Abingdon, 2006), 118.

6. Townsend and Bagby, *Suicide*, 118–19.

7. Townsend and Bagby, *Suicide*, 119.

8. All quotes come from my notes taken during the livestream of Cheslie Kryst's public memorial on February 18, 2022. At the time of her death, Kryst had written a memoir that included her struggles with depression. Her mother added to it, sharing her experience of her daughter's passing. Cheslie Kryst and April Simpkins, *By the Time You Read This: The Space between Cheslie's Smile and Mental Illness* (New York: Forefront Books, 2024).

9. Theologian and clinical psychologist Chanequa Walker-Barnes explores the myth of what she calls the "StrongBlackWoman" and discusses how depression and anxiety may present in Black women, in *Too Heavy a Yoke: Black Women and the Burden of Strength* (Eugene, OR: Cascade, 2014). A moving first-person account of a Black woman's depression is Nana-Ama Danquah, *Willow Weep for Me: A Black Woman's Journey through Depression*, 25th anniversary ed. (New York: Norton, 2023).

10. "Suicide Rates among Black Women and Girls Have Climbed for Two Decades," Columbia University Mailman School of Public Health, December 6, 2023, https://tinyurl.com/4tddszhe.

11. Coleman, *Bipolar Faith*, 333.

12. Seth Abruten and Anna S. Mueller, "Are Suicidal Behaviors Contagious in Adolescence? Using Longitudinal Data to Examine Suicide Suggestion," *American Sociological Review* 79, no. 2 (April 2014): 224. As the authors note, their research shows that Émile Durkheim's well-known assertion that strong social networks protect against suicide is not always correct.

13. Samuel Wells, ed., *Liturgy on the Edge: Pastoral and Attractional Worship* (Norwich, UK: Canterbury Press, 2018), 41. The chapter "Time to Talk" gives detailed suggestions for designing and hosting such a liturgy.

14. Wells, *Liturgy on the Edge*, 42.

15. Wells, *Liturgy on the Edge*, 43–44.

Bibliography

Abruten, Seth, and Anna S. Mueller. "Are Suicidal Behaviors Contagious in Adolescence? Using Longitudinal Data to Examine Suicide Suggestion." *American Sociological Review* 79, no. 2 (April 2014): 211–26.

Alter, Robert. *The Book of Psalms: A Translation with Commentary*. New York: Norton, 2007.

———. *The Hebrew Bible*. Vol. 2, *Prophets: A Translation with Commentary*. New York: Norton, 2019.

Ambrose of Milan. "On Virgins: Letter to Marcellina." Ethics of Suicide Digital Archive, May 21, 2015. https://tinyurl.com/5yexdzj5.

Antus, Elizabeth L. "'The Silence of the Dead': Remembering Suicide Victims and Reimagining the Communion of Saints." *Theological Studies* 81, no. 2 (2020): 394–413.

"Attempters' Longterm Survival." Harvard T. H. Chan School of Public Health. Accessed July 17, 2024. https://tinyurl.com/3rnuyvmw.

Augustine. *Concerning the City of God against the Pagans*. Translated by Henry Bettenson. New York: Penguin Classics, 1984.

———. "On Free Choice of the Will." Ethics of Suicide Digital Archive, May 21, 2015. https://tinyurl.com/3rwkthdb.

Bibliography

Baldwin, James. *Early Novels and Stories*. New York: Library of America, 1998.

Ball, Charles. *Slavery in the United States: A Narrative of the Life and Adventures of Charles Ball*. New York: John S. Taylor, 1837.

Bamford, Maria. *Sure, I'll Join Your Cult: A Memoir of Mental Illness and the Quest to Belong Anywhere*. New York: Gallery Books, 2023.

Bateson, John. *The Final Leap: Suicide on the Golden Gate Bridge*. Oakland: University of California Press, 2012.

Baumgaertner, Emily. "U.S. Rate of Suicide by Firearm Reaches Record Level." *New York Times*, November 30, 2023. https://tinyurl.com/bdcsmmjv.

Cabanatuan, Michael. "Golden Gate Bridge Board OKs $76 Million for Suicide Barrier." *SFGate*, June 28, 2014. https://tinyurl.com/mrxhca9d.

Catechism of the Catholic Church. Vatican City: Libreria Editrice Vaticana, 1993.

Catherine of Siena. *The Dialogue: A Conversation with God on Living Your Spiritual Life to the Fullest*. Gastonia, NC: TAN Books, 2010.

Coblentz, Jessica. *Dust in the Blood: A Theology of Life with Depression*. Collegeville, MN: Liturgical Press, 2022.

Coleman, Monica A. *Bipolar Faith: A Black Woman's Journey with Depression and Faith*. Minneapolis: Fortress, 2016.

Croy, N. Clayton. "'To Die Is Gain' (Philippians 1:19–26): Does Paul Contemplate Suicide?" *Journal of Biblical Literature* 122, no. 3 (Autumn 2003): 517–31.

Danquah, Nana-Ama. *Willow Weep for Me: A Black Woman's Journey through Depression*. 25th anniversary ed. New York: Norton, 2023.

Day, Dorothy. "On Pilgrimage." *Catholic Worker*, April 1948, 1, 2, 11.

Bibliography

Droge, Arthur J. "Mori Lucrum: Paul and Ancient Theories of Suicide." *Novum Testamentum* 30, no. 3 (July 1988): 263–86.

Eder, Steve. "As a Crisis Hotline Grows, So Do Fears It Won't Be Ready." *New York Times*, March 13, 2022. https://tinyurl.com/fk3ap77c.

The Episcopal Church. *The Book of Common Prayer and Administration of the Sacraments and Other Rites and Ceremonies of the Church: Together with the Psalter or Psalms of David according to the Use of the Episcopal Church*. New York: Church Publishing, 1979.

———. *The Book of Occasional Services 2022*. New York: Church Publishing, 2022.

Finnegan-Hosey, David. *Christ on the Psych Ward*. New York: Church Publishing, 2018.

Forest, Jim. *All Is Grace: A Biography of Dorothy Day*. Maryknoll, NY: Orbis Books, 2011.

Glaude, Eddie S., Jr. *Begin Again: James Baldwin's America and Its Urgent Lessons for Our Own*. New York: Crown, 2020.

Greene-McCreight, Kathryn. *Darkness Is My Only Companion: A Christian Response to Mental Illness*. Grand Rapids: Brazos, 2006.

Hari, Johann. *Lost Connections: Why You're Depressed and How to Find Hope*. London: Bloomsbury, 2018.

Heckler, Richard A. *Waking Up Alive: The Descent, the Suicide Attempt & the Return to Life*. New York: G. P. Putnam's Sons, 1994.

Hooff, Anton J. L. van. "A Longer Life for 'Suicide': When Was the Latin Word for Self-Murderer Invented?" *Romanische Forschungen* 102, no. 2/3 (1990): 255–59.

Houston, R. A. *Punishing the Dead? Suicide, Lordship, and Community in Britain, 1500–1830*. Oxford: Oxford University Press, 2010.

Hughes, Robert. *The Fatal Shore: The Epic of Australia's Founding*. New York: Vintage Books, 1988.

Bibliography

Jacobs, Harriet. *Incidents in the Life of a Slave Girl*. 1861. Reprint, Mineola, NY: Dover Thrift Editions, 2001.

Jamison, Kay Redfield. *Night Falls Fast: Understanding Suicide*. New York: Knopf, 1999.

Jennings, Willie James. *Acts*. Louisville: Westminster John Knox, 2017.

———. *The Christian Imagination: Theology and the Origins of Race*. New Haven: Yale University Press, 2010.

Keefe, Rachel A. *The Lifesaving Church: Faith Communities and Suicide Prevention*. Des Peres, MO: Chalice, 2018.

Kriner, Tiffany Eberle. *In Thought, Word, and Seed: Reckonings from a Midwest Farm*. Grand Rapids: Eerdmans, 2023.

Kryst, Cheslie, and April Simpkins. *By the Time You Read This: The Space between Cheslie's Smile and Mental Illness*. New York: Forefront Books, 2024.

Lee, Rhonda Mawhood. "Indissoluble." In *Common Prayer: Reflections on Episcopal Worship*, edited by Joseph S. Pagano and Amy E. Richter, 4–11. Eugene, OR: Cascade, 2019.

———. *Seek and You Will Find: Discovering a Practice of Prayer*. Cincinnati: Forward Movement, 2021.

Luther, Martin. "Table Talk." Entry 222 (April 7, 1532). Ethics of Suicide Digital Archive, May 21, 2015. https://tinyurl.com/yk3vvmu4.

Marchenko, Gillian. *Still Life: A Memoir of Living Fully with Depression*. Downers Grove, IL: InterVarsity Press, 2016.

Martin, Clancy. *How Not to Kill Yourself: A Portrait of the Suicidal Mind*. New York: Pantheon, 2023.

Mason, Karen. *The Essentials of Suicide Prevention: A Blueprint for Churches*. Eugene, OR: Cascade, 2023.

"Mental Health." World Health Organization, June 17, 2022. https://tinyurl.com/2a52n6ak.

Bibliography

Morrison, Toni. *Song of Solomon*. New York: Knopf, 1977.

Murray, Alexander. "Suicide in the Middle Ages." *Synergy* 18, no. 5 (Fall/Winter 2012): 1, 3–5.

———. *Suicide in the Middle Ages*. Vol. 1, *The Violent against Themselves*. Oxford: Oxford University Press, 1998.

———. *Suicide in the Middle Ages*. Vol. 2, *The Curse on Self-Murder*. Oxford: Oxford University Press, 2000.

"National Survey on LGBTQ Mental Health 2021." Trevor Project. https://tinyurl.com/3mcfxe4h.

Norris, Kathleen. *Acedia & Me: A Marriage, Monks, and a Writer's Life*. Reprint, New York: Riverhead Books, 2010.

Oberman, Heiko A. *Luther: Man between God and the Devil*. Translated by Eileen Walliser-Schwarzbart. New Haven: Yale University Press, 1989.

Palmer, Parker J. *Let Your Life Speak: Listening for the Voice of Vocation*. San Francisco: Jossey-Bass, 2000.

———. "My Spiritual Journey." *Patheos*, November 18, 2020. https://tinyurl.com/2ka5mrfa.

"Pastors Have Congregational and, for Some, Personal Experience with Mental Illness." Lifeway Research, August 2, 2022. https://tinyurl.com/bdzfeuhv.

Paulsen, David. "Visit to Castle's Dungeon in Ghana Offers ACC Lessons on Church's Complicity in the Transatlantic Slave Trade." Episcopal News Service, February 15, 2023. https://tinyurl.com/mr29sf4k.

Pierce, Yolanda. *In My Grandmother's House: Black Women, Faith, and the Stories We Inherit*. Minneapolis: Broadleaf Books, 2021.

Piersen, William D. *From Africa to America: African American History from the Colonial Era to the Early Republic, 1526–1790*. New York: Twain Publishers, 1996.

Bibliography

Rediker, Marcus. *The Slave Ship: A Human History*. New York: Penguin Books, 2008.

"Risk and Protective Factors for Suicide." Centers for Disease Control and Prevention. Accessed July 17, 2024. https://tinyurl.com/5n765y6e.

"Safe Reporting Guidelines for Media." American Foundation for Suicide Prevention. Accessed July 17, 2024. https://tinyurl.com/2p4yrf9c.

Seiden, R. H. "Where Are They Now? A Follow-Up Study of Suicide Attempters from the Golden Gate Bridge." *Suicide and Life-Threatening Behavior* 8, no. 4 (Winter 1978): 203–16.

Sheftall, Arielle H. "The Tragedy of Black Youth Suicide." *American Association of Medical Colleges News*, April 11, 2023. https://tinyurl.com/4ytujr3t.

Shneidman, Edwin S. *The Suicidal Mind*. New York: Oxford University Press, 1996.

Snyder, Terri L. *The Power to Die: Slavery and Suicide in British North America*. Chicago: University of Chicago Press, 2015.

Stevenson, Lisa. *Life beside Itself: Imagining Care in the Canadian Arctic*. Oakland: University of California Press, 2014.

Stuart, Kathy. *Suicide by Proxy in Early Modern Germany: Crime, Sin, and Salvation*. Cham, Switzerland: Palgrave Macmillan, 2023.

———. "Suicides by Proxy: The Unintended Consequences of Public Executions in Eighteenth-Century Germany." *Central European History* 41, no. 3 (September 2008): 413–45.

"Suicide." World Health Organization, August 28, 2023. https://tinyurl.com/3e9wdm8r.

"Suicide Data and Statistics" (2021). Centers for Disease Control and Prevention. https://tinyurl.com/yzjzn556.

"Suicide Rates among Black Women and Girls Have Climbed for

Two Decades." Columbia University Mailman School of Public Health, December 6, 2023. https://tinyurl.com/4tddszhe.

Talaga, Tanya. *All Our Relations: Indigenous Trauma in the Shadow of Colonialism*. London: Scribe, 2020.

Thomas Aquinas. *Summa Theologiae*. New Advent. Accessed July 17, 2024. https://tinyurl.com/5n6j5f6r.

Townsend, Loren L., and Daniel G. Bagby, eds. *Suicide: Pastoral Responses*. Nashville: Abingdon, 2006.

Walker-Barnes, Chanequa. *Too Heavy a Yoke: Black Women and the Burden of Strength*. Eugene, OR: Cascade, 2014.

Wells, Samuel, ed. *Liturgy on the Edge: Pastoral and Attractional Worship*. Norwich, UK: Canterbury Press, 2018.

"What We've Learned through Research." American Foundation for Suicide Prevention. Accessed July 17, 2024. https://tinyurl.com/2fs4xrmt.

Williams, Delores S. *Sisters in the Wilderness: The Challenge of Womanist God-Talk*. Maryknoll, NY: Orbis Books, 1993.

Winner, Lauren F. *Wearing God: Clothing, Laughter, Fire, and Other Overlooked Ways of Meeting God*. New York: HarperOne, 2015.

Further Resources

Beyond the resources listed in the bibliography, here are a few others I have found helpful.

Barbara Kopple's documentary *Running from Crazy* (2013), about Mariel Hemingway's exploration of mental illness and suicide in her family. It introduced me to the American Foundation for Suicide Prevention's annual Out of the Darkness Overnight Walk, which I completed in 2016.

Norah Vincent, *Adeline: A Novel of Virginia Woolf* (2016), explores the writer's life and death with a particular insight that Vincent, who was herself depressed and suicidal as she wrote, offers. Vincent availed herself of medically assisted death in Switzerland in 2022.

Matt Haig's novel *The Midnight Library* explores a suicidal mind and the myriad ways human lives are interconnected, whether or not we recognize those connections.

Stephen Daldry's 2002 film, *The Hours*, inspired by Virginia Woolf's novel *Mrs. Dalloway*, explores the theme of constrained freedom in choosing life or death.

Further Resources

Joan Wickersham's memoir, *The Suicide Index: Putting My Father's Death in Order* (2008), chronicles her quest to make sense of her father's—to her—nonsensical death.

Delphine de Vigan's novelized family history, *Nothing Holds Back the Night* (2014), tells the story of her mother's struggle with mental illness and her suicide, in a family marked by incest, accidental death, and other traumas.

Kate Bowler's "Everything Happens" podcast offers a helpful episode, "Suicide Prevention and Hope," with Pamela Morris-Perez, a psychologist whose adolescent daughter died by suicide: https://katebowler.com/podcasts/suicide-prevention-and-hope/.

The American Foundation for Suicide Prevention's resources, trainings, and support groups are invaluable.